THE ARCTIC WOLF
LIVING WITH THE PACK

L. David Mech
Foreword by Roger Caras

VOYAGEUR PRESS

Published by Voyageur Press, Inc.
123 North Second Street
Stillwater, MN 55082 U.S.A.

ISBN 0-89658-099-7

88 89 90 91 92 5 4 3 2 1

Printed in Singapore by Singapore National Printers Ltd
through Four Colour Imports, Ltd., Louisville K Y.

Because wolves are potential predators on nests of long-tailed jaegers, the birds regularly dive bomb the animals.

Dedicated to Dr. Durward L. Allen

Thirty years ago, Dr. Durward L. Allen of Purdue University helped launch me on my career as a wolf biologist. When he asked me to begin the study of wolves and moose on Isle Royale for my Ph.D. degree, I trust he had reason to believe I was suitable for the assignment. However, I doubt that Durward fully realized how ideally suited the assignment was for me.

Durward was already one of the leading wildlife biologists of his time when he learned about the unique natural experiment in progress on Isle Royale. He immediately set out to make certain that the experiment would be given scientific scrutiny. In so doing, he added to his very impressive set of scientific, educational, and literary accomplishments an achievement singular to the entire field of predator/prey relations.

Durward Allen set the Isle Royale wolf study in motion, monitored it, and participated in it through the tenures of several graduate students and associates. However, he also stepped back and allowed students of the Isle Royale ecosystems the freedom to develop their approaches in their own ways. He documented the first years of the still ongoing investigation in his delightful book, *The Wolves of Minong.*

Now, three decades after initiating the Isle Royale study, Durward Allen must be eminently pleased with the results of his insight. The world now knows without doubt that wolves can live with their prey under many environmental conditions. And although the moose/wolf scales sometimes tip precariously, they keep swinging back. By implication, then, the wolf comes out, to those who make judgments about the worth of creatures, a little bit better. Durward, serious scientist that he is, may not admit it, but I bet that secretly he's pleased.

For his invaluable contribution to our knowledge of wolves and for his role in starting me along the long trail that led inexorably to the wolf pack in the High Arctic, I am pleased to dedicate this book to Durward Allen.

Mom squeaks to the pups, and they swarm around her nipples to suckle.

4

CONTENTS

Foreword   *6*

Acknowledgments   7

Introduction   *8*

Lifetime Dream   *11*

To the High Arctic   *19*

White Wolves of the Ice   *25*

Search for the Den   *33*

Triumph   *39*

Second Thoughts   *45*

The Family   *51*

At Home with the Arctic Wolf   *57*

The Great Musk Ox Hunt   *69*

Return to the Family   *91*

On the Hunt   *99*

Survival of the Fittest   *107*

On Knowing the Wolf   *121*

Wolf Organizations   *122*

Suggested Readings   *125*

Index   *126*

FOREWORD

The wildlife crisis now gripping the natural world in the despair of escalating extinctions creates imperatives that were less apparent in times past. They have been part of the natural scene for centuries; but it is only now, on the eve of a night that will never end, that the urgency of these affairs is upon us, and the absolute necessity that we at last take action.

One of the most significant species, surely, is the wolf. Humans must learn to understand the wolf, for not only are these few subspecies clinging to the last edge of being, dangling over the void of nothingness forever, but the wolf in its remaining forms is a hallmark animal. If we cannot bring ourselves to understand the wolf, we probably will be able to understand little else.

Why the wolf? It is a predator like us. So far, humans have hated the wolf for just that unmistakable resemblance. We can find a way of co-surviving with the wolf only by forgiving it for being so like us. And the wolf first requires our understanding if that wisdom and compassion are to be found for it. Without human wisdom and compassion, nothing will survive.

One of the best ways of coming to understand the wolf is to listen to people like the author of this book. David Mech is a skilled and patient observer. In two years, studying one High Arctic pack, he gained further insight into the marvelous ways these animals bond to each other and to their habitat. Working hard, as all predators must work, Mech's

wolves wasted little, killed out of absolute necessity, and fit into a plan so complex, so perfect, we will yet be years in deciphering it.

In recent decades there have been special people like David Mech who have spent the time, endured the discomforts, to study animals in the only place it really matters, in their wild places. What Jane Goodall is to the chimpanzees of Gombe, David Mech has been for years to the wolf; what George Schaller was to the gorilla and is to the giant panda, Dr. Mech is to the wolf. There were Fossey and her gorillas, Kruuk and the hyena, Strum and the baboon, Moss and the elephants—names and species that are now permanently linked, not only in natural history literature but in the history of humans and nature and in the saga of people's efforts to reverse millenia of neglect.

If we do not follow the leadership of these field researchers and come to understand animals on the brink, there can be little doubt that we will follow those species over the edge. That is the ultimate observation, and it is inevitable. Most of the vertebrate species that have evolved on this planet are already extinct, and the rest stand poised for a signal from us. It is stay or go. The decision can be made only once for the species we have left. Here, at least, is a book that can help each of us understand what we stand to lose if we make the wrong decision.

Roger Caras

ACKNOWLEDGMENTS

Many people deserve mention for valuable assistance with the logistical aspects of my field trips, including especially G. Hobson, Polar Continental Shelf Project; D. Stossel, Atmospheric and Environmental Services, Environment Canada; Terry and Bezal Jesudasen, High Arctic International; J. Brandenburg and S. Durst, National Geographic Society; and R. Kellar, Bradley Air J. Brandenburg also helped me obtain the assignment that took me to the High Arctic and collaborated with me in working with the wolf pack. In addition, he and S. Durst were helpful and amiable companions during the parts of the field work we shared. D. Heard, J. Hunter, M. Ferguson, and their associates in the Wildlife Department of the Northwest Territories facilitated issuing permits for this study. The following individuals cooperated with various logistical problems: D. Bitton, F. Choquette, T. DeVeaux, and D. Jones. To all of the above I extend my heartfelt thanks.

I also owe a special debt to Ed Hickey of St. Lawrence, Newfoundland, for his open, friendly, and valuable cooperation.

INTRODUCTION

Last May, when David Mech asked me to write an introduction to his book on arctic wolves, he pointed out that another month would mark the thirtieth "anniversary" of the beginning of his career as a wolf biologist. It jolted me to realize that this was indeed the case. It was in late June 1958 that he and I journeyed north from the Purdue campus at West Lafayette, Indiana, to meet with an advisory committee in Isle Royale National Park.

About ten years before, a few wolves had crossed the ice from Canada and become established on the Lake Superior island—the northernmost land in Michigan. It was time for someone to make the most of this best-yet situation for predation research.

Later we could say that Dave's three-year study of the wolf and its prey turned out largely in accord with our speculative planning. It was the first in a series of projects that in this thirtieth year is still in progress. His doctoral thesis was published in the National Parks Fauna Series, and it was the second such "fauna" on the wolf. Previous to the Isle Royale work, our principal source of biological information in this field was *The Wolves of Mount McKinley*, by Adolph Murie, which had appeared in 1944.

Wolf relationships to Dall sheep and caribou in the Alaskan park would surely be different from the dynamics of predation on the moose of Isle Royale, but Murie's work undoubtedly would be helpful. The committee that met with us were not experts on the wolf; they were simply the best that could be mustered at the time. After several days of discussions, Dave and I took to the trails on our first field trip.

My acquaintance with Mech dated from the previous fall and a lecturing visit to Cornell University. I told the wildlife staff that I was looking for a graduate student of exceptional abilities—a capable scholar who could take care of himself in the woods. On Isle Royale we were groping our way, and such a man would be essential. I was quickly informed that one of the Cornell seniors abundantly met our requirements. L. David Mech (he pronounces it *meech*) was earning his way through school. He was an excellent student. He had three summers' experience as a field assistant in the New York bear project, which involved live-trapping and marking the bruins for ecological studies. His winter vacations were spent on snowshoes in the Adirondacks trapping fishers for their fur.

I was much impressed with Dave. He was lean and hungry. He had a frugal acceptance of whatever hardships outdoor living might require and a near-mystical curiosity about the complexities of nature. He responded in breathless incredulity to what I was offering—an opportunity to study wolves in an authentic roadless wilderness. We quickly came to terms.

The park staff were strongly supportive of the research; in effect they made it possible. In field aspects of the project, Dave was largely alone during the first two years. Summers were devoted mainly to fact-finding on moose and beavers, the food mainstays of the wolves. For seven weeks in February and March a camp was open on the otherwise deserted island. By means of a light plane on skis, the wolves could be observed from the air. As a vital contribution to the island program, Dave discovered Donald E. Murray, who would continue as our pilot, friend, and critical observer for twenty winters.

Through personal experiment, Dave and Don determined that the wolves would not attack a biologist who interrupted their feeding on a moose carcass. Himself immune to airsickness, Don helped his passenger endure the agonies of close-in circling over a kill. With woefully inadequate equipment, Dave thrust himself into the searing cold of the airstream to take pictures of events below; several of these were published in *National Geographic*.

Fortified by this conditioning and a new Ph.D., in 1962 Dave betook himself to Minnesota, the only state south of Canada with a major population of wolves. At the university he took courses for a year and became a research associate in the radio-tracking laboratory. Teaching and research at Macalaster College followed, and that was his base while he worked on his book *The Wolf: Ecology and Behavior of an Endangered Species*, published in 1970. For Dave and his family, these were times of "poverty level" living, but he had his eye on a better future.

That future began to unfold in 1969 when the U.S. Fish and Wildlife Service, in cooperation with the Forest Service and the state government, established the Minnesota wolf research program. Mech was put in charge and holds that position today, steadily extending his purview in wolf and large-animal biology and in the public-service aspects of his institutional duties. The work has included economic relationships of wolves in farm/forest borderlands — a principal interest of Dave's former student Steven H. Fritts. Dave takes pleasure in noting that his former student has come along — Fritts is now section leader of the federal endangered species program and Mech's immediate supervisor.

The Minnesota wolf studies have attracted public participation, independent support, and able scientific cooperators. Technical contributions of inestimable value have been made by Ulysses S. Seal, physiologist-biochemist (and much more) of the Veterans Administration and the University of Minnesota. Seal accompanied Dave to India, where they assisted national authorities on problems of immobilizing elephants and on radio-tracking the last of India's wild lions in the Gir Forest.

In 1985, Dave and others undertook plans for an international wolf center at Ely, with the mission of public information and education. They do not yet have a building, but the work is going forward. As an index of citizen attitudes and a credit to Minnesota legislators, a state grant of $200,000 to the wolf center became available last July.

Dave's imaginative field work on the arctic wolves, and this book as a personalized account of it, bear witness to what ardent effort and total dedication can accomplish. They clearly add to his distinction as a world authority in his chosen field. Most particularly, I have no doubt that he is now the only living person who has had his boot laces untied by a wild wolf.

Durward L. Allen
Purdue University
1 August 1988

LIFETIME DREAM

It was the highlight of my life. Hundreds of miles north of Hudson Bay, a thousand or more from the nearest city, I stood alone in the High Arctic—surrounded by wolves. No question, I had just discovered their den of pups, and they were only fifty feet away. All my searching had paid off. All the hard hours of hiking, all the planning, the hoping and the dreaming. After twenty-eight years, I had finally scored The Big One.

It wasn't that I had never found a wolf den before. In fact, I had found many. However, I had located all of them from an airplane, and they were all in forested areas. To watch them there, one would have to get so close that the wolves would spook and move the pups. Not so, here on the barren ground. Not only can you see forever here, but there really is no place to which the wolves can move their pups. Vegetation is sparse, and plants rarely grow higher than an inch or two. Permafrost prevents the mere digging of a den in the nearest hillside. Another den I had seen in the High Arctic apparently had been dug over a period of years up into a river bank, and still was only three feet deep.

My den was different. It was a cave under a beautiful orange-beige conglomerate rock outcrop. The most romantic artist could not have conceived a more scenic den. But except in the vicinity of this one, I never found another rock cave. Thus I suspected this den had been used for hundreds of years, and I later gathered some evidence for this notion.

So what's the big deal about getting close to a wolf den? Why should that be a highlight of anyone's lifetime? Did it merely seem sensational because I had

been living a pretty dull life?

On the contrary. I had already led what many people would think was a full and exciting life: catching and tying up black bears to be drugged and studied in the Adirondack Mountains; radio-tracking leopards in Kenya; darting lions in Tanzania; radio-tagging elephants, tigers, and several other exotic species in India; photographing caribou on the arctic tundra; counting ibex in the Soviet Union; and studying many other kinds of wild animals in several areas of the world. And these were merely side trips, that is, special assignments that punctuated my regular life. My actual job for twenty-eight years had been as a full-time wolf biologist, studying wolves on Isle Royale, and in Minnesota, Alaska, Italy, Portugal, and elsewhere.

And that was one of the reasons why this was such a special occasion for me—I was an obsessed student of wolves. Another reason was that watching wolves as closely as I had hoped to do with these animals had never been done before. Wolves are very intriguing animals, but difficult to get to know. They are the ancestor of the dog, but generally they are quite wild. Associating in packs, they travel far and wide in remote wilderness areas, and they live in very low densities, usually one pack per one hundred to eight hundred square miles. Originally they inhabited all of the northern hemisphere from the latitude of Mexico City and southern India northward to the North Pole.

However, because wolves kill and eat primarily large mammals—deer, elk, moose, caribou, bison, mountain goats, mountain sheep, and such—they

Two of the pack's adults stand guard near the den.

11

also sometimes prey on livestock. Thus many highly settled countries have exterminated wolves from much of their area. The animals are now gone from Mexico and most of the forty-eight contiguous United States except Minnesota. Montana, Wisconsin, Michigan, and perhaps Idaho all together contain less than sixty wolves.

Wolves are also missing from most of western Europe. Exceptions are Italy, Spain, and Portugal. Norway and Sweden support less than a dozen, although Finland and eastern Europe still harbor sizable numbers. The Mideast, Soviet Union, China, and central Asia also contain wolves in their more remote areas. Canada, which is still mostly wild and inaccessible, harbors one of the highest populations of wolves.

Wolves have been persecuted in so many areas that they remain only in remote wilderness. Thus they are very secretive and hard to study. The public doesn't always appreciate this fact; various books and movies, purporting to be true, have misled people about the ease of getting to know wild wolves. Even most of the many beautiful pictures of wolves that illustrate magazine articles, books, and posters are of captive wolves or of wolves people raised and temporarily released into the wild just to take their pictures. (One of the best examples of the latter approach can be seen in the book *The World of the Wolf*, which contains one of the finest collections of photos I've seen of wolves in a natural setting.) The number of unstaged wolf photos not taken from an aircraft has been very small — one more reason why I was so elated when I discovered this wolf den.

Because wolves are so difficult to approach in the wild, the traditional methods of studying them have mostly been indirect, such as tracking them in the snow and figuring out what they did; collecting and analyzing their droppings to determine diet; examining carcasses taken by hunters and trappers; observing the animals from aircraft; live-trapping, radio-tagging, and radio-tracking them; and studying captives.

Locating a wolf den and watching the pups and adults around it had long been one of my life's aspirations. As a teen I discovered a den of red foxes and was thrilled by just seeing the pups. I hoped to spend many days watching the den, but the day after I found it, a farmer plowed it up.

I did my first wolf study as a graduate student in Isle Royale National Park, a large Michigan island in northern Lake Superior, covering some 210 square miles. There, from 1958 through 1961, I spent three winters watching wolves from aircraft as they hunted moose. During summers I collected droppings and searched for dens. I found plenty of droppings but no dens.

While doing my background reading to prepare for the Isle Royale study, I had read the classic wolf book of its day, Adolph Murie's *The Wolves of Mt. McKinley*. Murie spent hours watching a den from a long distance through a spotting scope and thereby discovered that the pack is basically a family of adults and their offspring. His long-range descriptions of the home life of the pack fired my imagination as I began preparing for a career of studying wolves. I ached to watch a wolf den.

Such was not to be on Isle Royale, however. Even if I had found a den there, the brush and forest were so thick that I could never have watched from a distance, and the wolves would not have let me get close without moving their pups out of the area.

Later on, after I began wolf studies in Minnesota in 1966, I also fancied watching a den someday, although I would have to face the same problems as on Isle Royale. Nevertheless, when a local game warden told me the location of a den, I considered setting up a blind somehow and watching the wolves. One spring day I flew over the den and spotted adult wolves around freshly dug holes in a little clearing not too far from a small lake.

I hoped to be able to canoe across the lake without disturbing the animals and perhaps set up a blind in a swamp across the clearing from the den. In making my way in a few days later, however, I noticed something wrong with the den. I investigated and found that someone had dug out the pups. I later learned that it was the game warden, who sold the pups for $75 each. This was before the Endangered Species Act prohibited such activity.

By this time Farley Mowat's book *Never Cry Wolf* had appeared and was making quite a hit. The book, and the later movie of the same name, purported to be a true story of a hapless government biologist who lived near a wolf den in Canada and was more or less befriended by the wolves. The general public was taken by the idea and swallowed the story without question. Apparently no one thought to ask why a biologist and author who lived so intimately

The arctic wolf (Canis lupus arctos) is a subspecies or geographic race of the overall species called the gray wolf (Canis lupus) and is closely related to all other true wolves. However, arctic wolves are basically white, and they have more-rounded ears, a shorter muzzle, and shorter legs. Originally, scientists recognized twenty-four wolf subspecies in North America, including the eastern timber wolf, the northern Rocky Mountain wolf, the Mexican wolf, and others. In Europe and Asia, another eight subspecies are recognized. All subspecies can freely interbreed, and in most cases, only experts making many fine measurements on a large series of skulls can tell one race from another. Furthermore, scientists disagree considerably about which subspecies are really valid, and most believe that far too many subspecies are recognized in North America.

Adding to the confusion is the use of common names. For example, many laypeople refer to any wolf inhabiting forested areas as a timber wolf and any living north of the treeline as a tundra wolf, regardless of which geographic race the wolf is. Furthermore, the coyote (Canis latrans) is often called the brush wolf.

Additional confusion is generated by the red wolf of the southeastern U.S., which is technically known as Canis rufus. That means that, like the coyote, it is regarded as a fully separate species from the gray wolf. The dog (which was domesticated, by the way, from the wolf) is Canis familiaris, although many scientists consider it the same species as the wolf.

Neither the maned wolf (Chrysocyon brachyurus) of South America nor the Tasmanian wolf (Thylacinus cyncocephalus) of Tasmania is a true wolf.

with wolves never published a single picture of them. It was a truly delightful tale, but I learned from Canadian authorities and book reviews that it was not true. However, it certainly reinforced my own longing to at least watch a den.

I had published my own book, *Wolves of Isle Royale*, and was preparing a more complete work, *The Wolf*. While researching the literature I came across a most interesting article about an ornithologist who had encountered wolf pups in an area I had hardly heard of, "the High Arctic."

The High Arctic is the area north of the North American continent. The Arctic Circle runs at about 67 degrees north latitude, through northern Alaska, the Yukon Territories, and the Northwest Territories. When you get farther north of Alaska, beyond 70 degrees and especially beyond 75 degrees north latitude, you are in the High Arctic. A series of huge, barren islands fills the thousand-mile gap between the north edge of the continent and the North Pole. Some of the islands are even farther north than the Inuit live.

Lois Crisler's book *Arctic Wild* had described the arctic tundra of the Brooks Range in northern Alaska, where Lois and her husband Chris had hand-reared some wolf pups stolen for them by an Eskimo, or Inuk (plural, Inuit), from a den.

The Crislers raised the wolves on the tundra as part of a Disney film project, and Crisler's book details their life with these tame wolves out on the tundra. That was the kind of experience I would have given almost anything for. To think of traveling around with wolves out in the wild and watching them interact with their natural prey haunted me. But how many people would ever have a chance to hand-rear pups out in the wilderness?

Ever since I became interested in wolves I have known that in the High Arctic they are relatively unafraid of people. It is generally thought that this is because the wolves there have not been harassed by any kind of hunting. In the High Arctic, game is so sparse and conditions so severe most of the time that even Inuit seldom venture there. The northern-most native community is Grise Fiord on the south end of Ellesmere Island, at about 76 degrees north latitude, and even that village was established by the Canadian government with Inuit from farther south. It is totally dark for almost five months of the year.

Whatever the reason, wolves in the polar region respond quite differently to humans than elsewhere. For instance, Canadian caribou biologist Frank Miller, on his hands and knees, once lured a wolf in and fed it a candy bar on Melville Island. Another time, three paleontologists studying Ellesmere Island spotted a pack of six wolves closing in on them. Suddenly the lead wolf jumped up and, with its mouth, grazed the cheek of one of the workers. The pack then went on its way. Wolves do not attack humans, and this incident did not harm the scientist. Apparently the wolves were just curious.

However, the most incredible wolf/human experience I knew of had occurred to the ornithologist I mentioned earlier, Dr. David Parmelee, in the High Arctic. Back in 1955, he had run down a wolf pup on foot and was carrying it to his tent. His shotgun rested over his shoulder, with dead ptarmigan dangling by strings from it. Suddenly his partner told him to glance behind. "Following close in my footsteps was the big she-wolf; her nose touching the ptarmigan as they swayed back and forth. Incredible as it surely is, we several times had to drive that wolf off with snowballs for fear that we would lose our specimens."

I really envied Parmelee, along with Crisler and Murie. However, there was little I could do about it back in Minnesota.

Mom patrols the area around the pack's secondary den.

Polar bears prowl the shores of the High Arctic islands, searching for seals and other seafaring food.

Arctic wolf tracks dent the mud near a tundra stream. The front foot track (top) is wider than the rear.

16

A yearling male of the High Arctic pack howls in reply to his pack mates.

TO THE
HIGH ARCTIC

By 1968 I was radio-tagging wolves in Minnesota for the U.S. Fish and Wildlife Service. Then it was easy to locate dens from the air by homing in on the adult wolves while they were there, so I found several dens. I even saw pups from the air and watched them playing around the dens. Again, however, I was stymied in even attempting to do any serious observing of them from the ground. A few times I deliberately walked in fairly close to the den and actually spotted pups. However, they rarely stuck around for more than a few seconds before zipping into the den hole. I always retreated for fear that the adults would move the pups and jeopardize them. If I was ever going to watch a den, it would have to be somewhere above the treeline.

I thought my opportunity had come in 1973 when *National Geographic* asked me to write an article about wolves. The magazine was willing to fund a trip for me to expand my background into areas of wolf biology where I lacked experience. I thus chose to go to Bathurst Inlet, where, I had heard, the local Inuit knew of some dens. I was thrilled to finally trek the tundra, sit around on barren knobs, and watch for wolves and caribou over hundreds of square miles. Shades of Crisler and Murie, I hoped. My photographer Dave Hiser and I did spot a few wandering wolves, and we were shown where a pack had denned a few years earlier. However, the animals attending the dens had all been killed, so again, no den watching.

Another near miss at watching a wolf den came when a movie producer approached me to assist in making a movie about tundra wolves. The budget was large enough so that sufficient time and money were available to help ensure that an active den was located. Because of the press of other duties, I chose to assist with the filming during the second year of the project to allow more time for planning my schedule. Fortunately for the producer, but not for me, he completed the film, *Following the Tundra Wolf*, in the first year, including some great shots of pups around the den. In that case, most of the shooting was done from about a half mile away with long telephoto lenses, for the wolves were very shy of humans. I would love to have been able to watch even from that long a distance. No such luck, however.

Meanwhile, my appetite for the High Arctic increased. A Canadian biologist had written a master's thesis based on observing wolves around a den on Bathurst Island. Again it was from a blind, and at a long distance, but he did demonstrate that it could be done. Another biologist had published an article about the wolves around the area where Parmelee had encountered such tame individuals. This biologist too had been able to watch the wolves at close quarters. He even found their den, although he spent little time actually watching it. I had to get there.

As I continued full time with my wolf research in Minnesota, I was asked to set up a wolf study on the Kenai Peninsula of Alaska. In the process, I encountered a graduate student who was about to complete his master's thesis, based on a study of watching wolves around a den in the Arctic National Wildlife Refuge on the north slope of the Brooks Range of extreme northeastern Alaska. He persuaded me to take him on for a Ph.D. study involving the same den.

I accompanied the student to the area and finally

did get to observe wolves coming and going around the den for a few days. The hole itself was in a willow thicket on the side of a mountain, so it was difficult to see a great deal from a distance. However, the wolves got too upset when we came closer than about a half mile. Even though I finally had my big opportunity, I really was unable to cash in on it.

Soon after I left, a rabid wolf approached the others around the den and fought with them, and within a few weeks the pack was wiped out. Thus went any further opportunity for studying that den.

Since then, I really hadn't had any more wolf-den adventures or near-adventures, although I was always keeping my antennas up for possibilities. I'm not sure whether that was in the back of my mind when a photographer, Jim Brandenburg, suggested I propose to *National Geographic* writing an article about Ellesmere Island. Jim had been assigned to photograph the Steger/Schurke expedition to the North Pole. Because the expedition would be leaving from northern Ellesmere, he would have to spend time on the island anyway, and he thought he might photograph the island as well. The area was one where, I had known for almost twenty years, wolves tolerated humans. Who knows? Maybe I would run into such wolves. At the least I would be able to visit an obscure and little-known location on the globe. When I received the assignment, I leapt at the chance.

Just getting to within a thousand miles of the spot was an adventure. The trip involved flying from Montreal to Devon Island by commercial plane, a nine-hour flight. It might turn into an eighteen-hour one if the only airstrip on the island was socked in, for the alternative to landing was to return to Montreal. The plane was basically a cargo craft, with the last third of the body fitted for passengers, a colorful assortment of geologists, Inuit, a few tourists and adventurers, meteorologists, technicians, and other northern workers. On later flights there was often a beautiful woman, lending stark contrast to the scene. It was mid-April 1986, but the photographer and I quickly left spring behind in Montreal. Below us, the dark boreal forest blended increasingly with whiteness. Myriads of snow-covered frozen lakes that spotted the spruce/balsam blanket gave way to white expanses of snowy open ridges, with tinier and tinier trees poking up only in the low spots. After a few hours, the whiteness grew much more stark as trees disappeared and great portions of the Arctic Ocean stretched out on each side. Long rents in the ice exposed the coldest blue water I had ever seen.

A definite air of excitement pervaded the passengers. And it wasn't just the adventurers and sightseers jumping from window to window with their Nikons, recording the unique beauty of the frozen north below. Even the old Arctic hands—you could tell them by their highly experienced field clothes—began to buzz as we passed over the water. This was a coming-out again. Lovers of their work were returning to honeymoon after spending the winter in civilization, estranged. There's something about the Arctic that draws people back.

The end of the line was Resolute Bay, an Inuit village of perhaps 150 people. Fortunately the airport was open, so we didn't have to return to Montreal. We filed into the tiny terminal and sorted our bags. We were to overnight at High Arctic International, a friendly, homey tourist haven operated by Terry and Bezal Jesudasen. Whenever possible, we were to catch a chartered twin otter aircraft farther north on the last leg of our trip.

"Whenever possible" turned out to be a few days later, in the middle of the night. A blizzard had raged for two days. I was going crazy. Here we were in the High Arctic, and all we could do was stay indoors. I contented myself by periodic strolls outside to test my arctic gear.

First I tried my Minnesota loggers' heavy woolen pants, good to 50 below easily. But in the High Arctic those pants were thoroughly air conditioned. They probably would have been all right if it weren't for the wind, which blew right through them. The only solution was Bezal's windpants, which I promptly leased. Facemasks and snowgoggles were another problem. I had several varieties of both, so I tried various combinations. None worked, but one was better than the others.

My test zone was a local hill directly behind the village. The wind was pouring over the top so hard that it was very hard to climb against. When I got a third of the way up the hill, the tiny village disappeared in the fine, blowing snow below. On my return to the town, each trial run became a serious quest to find High Arctic International. I couldn't see more than about fifty feet, and every building was a blur through the blowing snow as seen

The massive face of a glacier moves slowly forward, scouring up boulders and scree as it goes.

When glaciers reach the sea, their ragged fronts float until pieces break off and form icebergs, a process known as calving.

through the frosted yellowish snowgoggles.

Even after determining the best combination of my entire arctic suit and testing it repeatedly, I continued to mount the village hill just for the exercise. I was dying to get out and do something.

Finally, the call came at about midnight of the third day. The blizzard was still raging, but we were to leave at 3:00 A.M. We were low enough in latitude that it was still dark in the middle of the night. Farther north, where we were bound, it would be light all day and night, even in April.

To cover the mile to the airport through the blowing and drifted snow, we had to use snowmobiles and sledges. The road was thoroughly obliterated. Bezal and an assistant prepared the machines for our expedition. In addition to all our gear, we had to take enough sleeping bags for all of us in case we got lost or conked out along the way to the airport. Thus the heavy wooden sledges were loaded with gear, and we each rode on one.

The only way for me to hold on to the sledge was by grabbing the south end of one of the 2 x 4 floor slats, and I clutched it firmly. Bezal was trying to follow the road by guiding on the periodic telephone poles along its north side. However, the wind was blowing from the north so hard that it kept pushing us toward the south side of the roadway. Iron rods of some sort stuck up there every fifty feet or so, and I noticed us heading perilously close to some of them. Each time Bezal tried to turn the snowmobile back toward the north side of the

road, my sledge would swing toward the south.

Suddenly I realized that if everything came together just right, my sledge might just clip up against one of those iron rods. There was no way I could signal Bezal, who might as well have been miles away. Thus I decided to release my grip on the outside edge of the sledge, just in case.

"*Crack*"—the sledge slammed up against a post and sliced along it, knocking me in the leg (heavily padded by my arctic windsuit) and throwing me from the sledge into the dark night and deep snow. But I was thankful. Had I waited a second more to move my hand, it wouldn't have been there.

We finally found the airport, loaded the plane, and took off. Because all the runways were clogged, we merely took off across a taxiway. The wind was strong enough that the takeoff was no problem for the mighty twin otter.

When I awoke a few hours later over one of the other High Arctic islands, everything was white—up, down, and ahead. The pilot, however, evidently could see some kind of airstrip, for he headed down. One finally materialized out of the whiteout as though suddenly conjured up. We put down and unloaded the gear, including snowmobiles, and the plane refueled from a gas cache for the flight to its next destination. I would headquarter here, at one of the few manned outposts in the High Arctic, and explore the surroundings.

The area was all barren and white, but I knew there was much to be seen. I just had to find it.

Even in August, much of the High Arctic remains frozen.

WHITE WOLVES
OF THE ICE

Much of the High Arctic is covered with glaciers and icefields; where it is not, mountains, hills, and plains of gravel prevail. The wind blows almost constantly, and for four to five months each year, darkness obscures the region for twenty-four hours per day. Thus the High Arctic is not a hospitable place for plants. The nearest tree grows more than a thousand miles to the south, and the tallest plant stands about six inches. Most plants in the area hug the ground, and they grow only in intermittent patches, usually on lowlands and wet hillsides. In April even those plants were snow-covered.

I, of course, was more interested in finding the animals that live on the plants, and the predators, especially the wolf, that feed on the vegetarians. Seven species of land mammal eke their living in this area, and eke they must. With vegetation so sparse, and covered with snow nine months of the year, the plant eaters—collared lemmings, arctic hares, Peary caribou, and musk oxen—must move almost constantly just to find enough to eat.

The first musk oxen I ever saw, for example, had disappeared by the next day, even though I could see over the snow-covered ground for miles. It was, however, clear from the musk oxen's tracks how the burly beasts garner their daily supply of sedges and willows. They frequent windblown plains, paw out the vegetation, munch it down, shuffle around a bit, and paw for more. When a herd of ten to fifteen musk oxen passes through, the snow is well disturbed and the vegetation well sampled.

No one knows how many musk oxen inhabit the region—it is too costly to do much of a survey that far north. I eventually counted 183 musk oxen on about nine hundred square miles of good range in 1986. This points up one of the ways musk oxen and other land mammals of the High Arctic make it— they live in relatively low densities and cover large areas.

During summer, musk oxen seem to favor the lower, wetter areas, where they rely primarily on willows and sedges. Caribou too feed on willows and sedges, but also include mosses and lichens in their diet. Caribou tend to frequent dryer sites, such as ridges and hillsides, although since they travel even more widely than musk oxen, they can be found in transit almost anywhere.

I will certainly never forget the first Peary caribou I ever saw. My partner was out ahead of me on his snowmobile, buzzing smoothly up a broad, snowy hillside, when suddenly he stopped and aimed his camera. I noticed some whitish creatures ahead of him and thought they might be wolves, since we had run into no sign of caribou in the region. Lifting my frosted snowgoggles, I looked again. One hundred fifty yards away stood five elfin caribou, white except for brownish backs and tiny antlers.

After a bit of maneuvering for pictures, we found that the caribou weren't the least bit afraid of us, and eventually we walked right up to them. Obviously young, they had an air of naiveté that almost made me wonder what they would have done had we been wolves.

Actually, I knew the answer—flee. That is the caribou's main defense against predators. But their success in using flight as an escape depends on their

The wolves liked to frequent an iceberg, which they climbed and explored regularly.

25

The musk ox is a shaggy beast, appearing for all the world like something out of the Stone Age.

Peary caribou are diminutive forms of their larger cousins, the woodland caribou, which inhabit the area a thousand miles to the south.

ability to discern precisely when to flee. In this case, they had judged that we weren't wolves or bears, and in their experience that was all that counted. Humans hadn't been a problem, at least in recent times. This area was 250 miles from the nearest hunters.

That is probably the reason that not only the caribou but the musk oxen, arctic hares, and supposedly even the wolves were so approachable—no real history of danger from humans, and so little exposure to them ever.

Except for the lemming, no doubt the most numerous mammal in the High Arctic is the arctic hare. Weighing up to twelve pounds, this white oversized bunny is quite prominent, especially since it lives in herds of up to a hundred or more. Like the musk oxen and caribou, the hare feeds to a great extent on arctic willow, pawing sprigs out from under the snow and sometimes scratching out even the roots. The animal then moseys on, nose twitching, until it discovers a new plant to devour.

In June and July, hares produce up to six young (leverets), which they then leave alone for long periods and nurse perhaps once per day. The leverets are a stony gray, precisely matching most of their surroundings. The moment they stop moving, they disappear.

The hare possesses a peculiar habit of standing on its hind legs, a trait that certainly serves it well in the High Arctic. Since hares generally frequent higher ground, these mobile lookout towers can detect a disturbance a mile or more away. If the disturbance takes the form of a large, four-legged animal with sharp teeth, the hare flees the vicinity. Its flight, however, is not your regular, run-of-the-mill bunny hop. Instead, the arctic hare uses a sophisticated gait known as "ricochetal" in scientific circles—it hops like a kangaroo, on its hind legs, dropping down on all fours only occasionally.

Such a gait certainly would help the hopping hare detect any wolves closing in from either side as it flees from the one behind it. Besides allowing hares to see farther when they run, their two-legged hop supposedly gives them much greater acceleration and maneuverability. It is interesting that when disturbed by an aircraft, hares also flee, but I have never seen one resort to its ricochetal gait at such a time.

The three meat-eating land mammals in the High Arctic—ermine, arctic fox, and wolf—depend on the other four species, and there must be even fewer of the predators than of the main plant-eaters they prey on. Of the three meat-eaters, we especially wanted to find the wolves.

We never did, however. They found us instead. Just as we returned from a scouting trip and were entering a little building at the outpost, I happened to look around behind me. A snowy driveway ran from my right to my left down a hill only fifty feet away, and just behind that rose a ridge. On the ridge stood seven wolves! I couldn't believe it. Right here at the outpost, like a pack of dogs!

When I thought about it later, it really didn't seem so unusual. The temperature was 30 degrees below zero, a strong wind was blowing, and windchill was probably minus 100 degrees. Thus the inhabitants of the base rarely ventured out. When they did, it certainly wasn't for long. Only extremely insulated and totally covered fools with some kind of a mission (like me) stayed out for long. The area around the buildings was really quite isolated and human-free for most of the year. The smell of food from the mess hall may have attracted the wolves. I also learned that the animals visited the outpost dump, as wolves, bears, foxes, and other wildlife do the world over.

Of course I was elated. Here in my own backyard was my primary quarry. If I worked things right, I might just be able to observe and photograph these wolves. However, just to make sure I didn't think my quest was going to be too easy, the wolves lumbered off down the hill, behind a couple more buildings, and out away from the outpost. They may not really have been too afraid of us, but at the same time, they didn't exactly trust us either. That would take time.

These wolves liked to hang around an iceberg frozen into the fjord not far from shore. One blustery night I was exploring the iceberg. The sun was already circling around the sky each day and night, destined to shine constantly for the next four months. Its rays this night provided a welcome solace against the frigid air. As I rounded a jagged corner of the gigantic ice chunk, I spied the wolves just heading around the other side. I hurriedly backtracked along my side toward where they should soon appear, hoping to ambush them.

The wolves were faster than I, however, and were already out on the fjord when I arrived at the other

Adult arctic hares may weigh as much as twelve pounds; they remain white even during summer in certain parts of the High Arctic.

Young arctic hares are cryptically colored; when they lie still, they disappear.

end of the iceberg. Nevertheless I lay flat on my belly and began whining as loudly as I could. With my heavily insulated windsuit, facemask, and sunglasses, I'm not sure what they thought I was, but at least I aroused their curiosity.

The wolves at the rear of the pack, now some hundred yards away, immediately turned around and began approaching me cautiously, their white shaggy fur flowing in the breeze. I tried a number of variations during the next several minutes, hoping to figure out what was the most alluring: crawling on belly, flopping around, crawling on hands and knees toward them, rolling sideways, and so on. Just lying flat and still and whining seemed to bring the best response.

Even the leader, a hundred yards ahead of the others, returned to the pack as they approached me. The closest any wolf got that time was about one hundred and fifty feet away, but it was quite a thrill anyway. I recalled the time many years ago when as a green graduate student I had hidden in a shanty on Isle Royale in Lake Superior one winter and ambushed a pack of fifteen wolves passing by. The feeling was the same, even though this time the wolves were farther away. Perhaps it was lying alone out on the ice instead of in a shack that made the experience so exhilarating this time.

Every chance we got, we would interact with the pack, try not to scare them, and try to reinforce them when they approached or stuck near us. Each time, we experimented with methods of approaching them and getting them used to us. After several days and nights of intensive effort, the wolves began to accept us. With continuous daylight and nowhere to hide in this bleak and snowy land, they had to come to terms with us or constantly run away.

Just before we had to leave we found ourselves fully accepted by the pack. On our snowmobiles, we could actually travel in among the wolves. We had almost become part of the pack! It was really sad to have to leave.

My only consolation was that I knew I would be returning in a couple of months, when I could arrange a more extensive vacation leave. Who knows what that trip might hold? By then the wolves should be denning. If they were to remember me, I might be able to realize my long-term goal of watching them raise their pups around their den. The den would probably be on some hillside, so I might be able to hide on a nearby hill and with binoculars spy on the wolves' most intimate behavior. I couldn't imagine a more ideal vacation.

The author in arctic gear ready to face windchills of minus l00 degrees, which are not uncommon in the High Arctic during April.

One of the first views the author had of his High Arctic family.

During Arctic windstorms, even wolves with their thick, shaggy coats must squint to forge ahead.

As the author and his partner acclimated the wolves, the animals allowed the men to travel on snowmobiles among them in the pack.

After more than twenty-five years of hoping, wishing, and dreaming, and a week more of solid searching, the author finally discovered this magnificent wolf den.

SEARCH FOR
THE DEN

I realized that the chances of my dream coming true were slim. First the wolves would have to have bred. Generally wolves do breed every year, but in the High Arctic so little is known about wolves that not much can be taken for granted. If they did breed, then the pups would have to survive, and that can be a problem for wolves anywhere. In addition, I would have to find the den. I knew that packs at this latitude probably traveled over home ranges perhaps thirty miles across. That's a lot of country to search.

Even if I did find a den of pups, there was no guarantee the wolves would remember me. Or if they did, they still might not allow me anywhere near the den. With their entire year's reproductive investment tied up in one litter of pups, they might be far more wary than they were during winter when they had little to lose by tolerating me. If I disturbed them, they might move the pups to some other spot. Worse yet, they might abandon the pups or kill them. Fortunately, no other biologists I knew of who had stumbled onto wolf dens had found that the wolves had killed or abandoned their pups as a result. Nevertheless, it does happen in captivity, so I knew I would have to be very careful.

These hopes and doubts had been on my mind when we left in April, and they were still strong when I returned alone in July. This time, along with a tent, sleeping bag, dried food, stove, and other camping gear, I also brought a three-wheeler to get around on. The snow in lowland areas was mostly gone, so the landscape had changed dramatically.

The first time I found a wolf and pulled up to it,

I was highly encouraged: The animal seemed to remember me. It acted just as the others had in winter and allowed me to approach to within a few yards. Maybe my plan to watch the den actually held some promise!

First I would have to find the den, and that would be a tremendous challenge even for me as a wolf biologist. I knew that the den should be on a hill or ridge near water. I presumed it would be some sort of hole in the ground, since there seemed to be no other possible type of shelter like there might be in forested areas—a hollow log, blown-down-tree roots, or an old abandoned beaver lodge.

I also knew that there should be a concentration of tracks funneling toward the den. As the adults hunted miles from the den, they would tend to beeline it back there with food. The closer I came to the den, the more concentrated the trails of tracks should be. Nevertheless, finding tracks on the tundra would not be easy.

It seemed like there were a million miles of tundra hummocks to search. Thus I concentrated on easier places like muddy river bars, creek beds, old military or survey roads, and musk ox trails. It seemed logical enough. Little did I realize, however, how far astray all my good planning was leading me.

Another technique I tried was to sit around on various high spots watching over the hundreds of square miles through binoculars to try to spot any white specks picking their way over the gravel and tundra. Eliminating arctic hares, which I quickly learned to distinguish, the other white specks would be wolves. Generally they would be traveling either

In warmer parts of the High Arctic, gravel and soil replace icefields and provide a thin base for low-growing plants, which then support the sparse animal community.

Icebergs of exquisite beauty dot the sea during the two months of summer in the High Arctic.

to or from the den. By combining enough such sightings, I might deduce the direction of the den. I would start near where we had seen the wolves in April, and then generally spread my efforts from there.

At first it seemed easy. I spied a few wolves on open hilltops and watched which direction they headed. A problem soon arose, however. The wolves would cover a few hundred yards, dip down over a ravine, and disappear, not to be seen again. It was not always the same hill or ravine, but there were enough such spots around that they seriously hampered my plan to figure out any single area to which the wolves were traveling. Of course, in half the cases, on the average, the animals would actually be heading *away* from the den, going hunting.

After a few days of more or less random searching, I reached a breakthrough. Parallel to a long fjord, an old road led to a river delta. The melting snow water had percolated down to the frost layer, leaving the upper few inches of soil soggy. There in the old muddy roadway lay a wolf superhighway, packed with tracks going both ways. The den had to be in one direction or the other, and that greatly narrowed my search area. The trouble was that the well-tracked trail went on for miles. Fortunately, the view from the trail toward the fjord was breathtaking. In the foreground, mats of purple saxifrage poked up through the gravel, while beyond, little white icebergs studded the deep blue water.

When the wolf tracks hit the river delta, they crossed the muddy flats and headed out across an extensive plain at the head of the fjord. Far in the background, white sawtooth mountains bordered the plain. As I surveyed the scene, I suddenly became dismayed. Had the wolves been concentrating their travels along the fjord merely to reach the head of it so they could make their way around it? Certainly it was too wide and cold to swim. Maybe the den was nowhere near.

As I looked around, my dismay turned to elation. At one side of the wide plain, in the direction of the tracks disappearing ahead of me, stood a large sandy hill a mile away. Just the kind of place where the wolves might den! The hill, being raised, would be well drained, so permafrost might not be such a problem. And sand, of course, would be easy to dig in.

To cross the river, I took off my boots, stuffed my heavy wool socks into them, hung them around my neck, rolled up my pants, and waded in. Glacier-cold water quickly numbed my feet, but the prospect of finding the den warmed my spirit enough to compensate. I found some respite on reaching each mud flat between the branches of the river. Finally emerging on the far side of the delta, I dried my wooden lower limbs with my shirt, pulled my boots on, and struck out along the wolf trail with great anticipation.

Sure enough, the tracks headed over toward one end of the hill. On the other hand, the wolf trails became more diffuse, the opposite of what I had expected. There were tracks here and there in the sand, but as I climbed the hill, I despaired at the lack of real trails. Still, the hill was worth searching. It was, after all, just the kind of place I was looking for. Moreover, if the den wasn't here, then the next nearest possibility in this direction was the mountain range perhaps another fifteen to twenty-five miles away. The wolves wouldn't dig a den on the lowland plain in between.

So search I did. The hill was about a half-mile long and a quarter-mile wide. Back and forth across the top I walked. Up one side and down the other. I searched every little ridge that protruded, and every gully. I found wolf tracks and droppings, old and fresh, and musk ox remains. In one spot along a gentle slope on one side of the hill, the scattered white bones of an adult musk ox kill lay half buried by drifting sand. Within twenty-five feet was the hair and stomach contents of a fresh calf kill, made perhaps a week or two before. A single frail rib bone and a chewed shoulder blade were the only other remains I could find.

Discovering the kill really piqued my interest. From a strictly objective standpoint, the kill actually told me nothing more than did a single fresh track or dropping—at least one wolf had recently been here. Nevertheless, something subjective about seeing fresh kill remains brought the scene to life. A few days ago, right here, at least one wolf, probably several—the wind had since obliterated their trails—had skirmished hard with a musk ox and calf, probably a herd. The calf had lost, and the wolves had eaten. And somewhere—I just had to find where—they had fed some of that food to the pups at the den.

But by this time I realized that the den probably

wasn't here. I finished searching the huge wide hill, just to be sure, but found no well-worn wolf trails or other evidence that the den was on the hill. Thus it had to be many miles away.

Descending to the plain and a wide mud flat at the head of the fjord, I sought confirmation that my alternative idea was correct, that the wolf highway was merely a funnel between the fjord and a mountain ridge paralleling it. If so, the wolf trails should fan out across the plains near the head of the fjord.

That's just what I found. And there was no one trail that seemed better used than any other. If there had been, I would have thought that the den was even farther beyond, in the long mountain range on the horizon. It could still be there, but I decided to check the possibility that it was back the other way, back toward where the funnel was pointing.

That area was dominated by huge hills intersected by steep ravines, narrow creek beds, and a wide river valley. An extensive plain stretched twenty miles to the north beyond the nearby hills and was bordered by other hills. There certainly was enough territory to search for a wolf den. Since I had no more good leads based on concentrations of wolf tracks, I decided again to emphasize watching for wolves and seeing which way they were going.

I already had seen wolves a couple of times heading in one certain direction, but they had quickly disappeared into a ravine. Of course, I had searched the ravine and every area around it where there might be a den, but found no further leads. Perhaps the den was way beyond. By positioning myself near where I had last seen the wolves, I might eventually find how they were leaving the ravine.

My biggest break came one evening when a shorter-legged gray-backed wolf trotted right by me, heading toward the place where the wolves I had seen earlier had disappeared. This animal stopped broadside of me, however, and let me scan it closely with binoculars. Two key points struck me. The wolf had well-developed nipples, and her belly was full. Translation: Here was the alpha female, she was nursing pups, and she was at this moment heading to the den to feed them.

Now I was really excited! This proved there were pups and a den. I had believed in it all along, but I certainly gained a strong boost when I finally found this living proof.

"Mom," as I later named her, was on a beeline. If I could just run along behind her, I'd soon be at the den — but that was out of the question. Even on a flat straightaway, I'd never be able to keep up, for wolves' regular rate of tireless travel is about five miles per hour; and if they are intent on any kind of goal at all, they are faster. Furthermore, Mom's route was directly down into the ravine, back up the other side, and over the hill, straight on her beeline. At the other end of the line, an unknown distance away, was my coveted goal.

Now, like a bloodhound, I would follow that line till I reached my quarry. Although the distance between where I first spotted Mom and where she disappeared was only a half mile, I could see on the horizon, many miles away, where the line fell that was formed by these two points. I could thus plot it on my map. It might still take many days, but I had no doubt now that I would find the den.

I had already thoroughly searched the hill over which Mom had vanished, so the den must be beyond that. The next day I alternately searched the region beyond and sat for hours watching further for wolves. Seeing one in this new area would save much hunting. I considered howling and listening for responses, a trick I often use elsewhere to help locate wolves. However, such howling ordinarily would be taken by the wolves as coming from an intruder, and in no way did I want to risk being so regarded. That could blow my whole plan.

It turned out I didn't need to howl. While sitting atop my three-wheeler on a minor ridge, scanning the slopes of a higher one to my left, I suddenly noticed a flash of white to my right, one hundred yards or so away. There, heading out on the beeline, were three wolves. Clearly I was closer to the den.

I swung around to the right to see through my binoculars whether Mom was with the pack. The wolves stopped. I suddenly wished I had been lying flat, for I didn't want to scare them. This was the first time the wolves had seen me so far from the outpost, and I thought they might become upset, especially if I was close to the den.

My fears were groundless. Almost like old friends who hadn't seen me for awhile, the wolves headed right over. Mom was not with them. One wolf came to within ten feet, while the others hung back a few yards more. I decided to toss them a few tidbits. The nearest jumped back a bit but returned, nosed the food tentatively, and ate it! I was in good standing with them.

Not wanting to push my luck, I remained motionless for a few minutes and let them leave with no negative interaction. They then continued sprightly on their way, apparently off on a hunt. I waited for ten minutes until they dropped over a bank and out of sight. I didn't want them to see my searching around their den.

My next step was to head to where the wolves had appeared. My every move now had to be slow, cautious, and deliberate. The den could be close, and I didn't want to stumble onto it and scare the pups or any adults left there. Where I had seen the wolves appear from behind a hill, I dismounted and checked for tracks and then began backtracking them. Because the area was covered with heathery hummocks that did not record tracks well, the problem was difficult.

However, knowing that wolves usually beeline, I was able to pick from muddy spot to muddy spot along that line and confirm their backtrack route: down a little valley where they had crossed a stream a foot and a half wide, then up the other side to a ridge. Slowly and cautiously I went, constantly looking around for a hole, a wolf, pups, or whatever first indication I might see of a den. My excitement mounted as I searched. I must be close.

I climbed a short ways up to a rocky ridge, and then I saw it — an old musk ox bone, and then another. Suddenly I realized I must be almost standing on a den. A series of small rock caves undermined the rocky ridge, and worn trails led in and out of them.

They were too small for adult wolves, so I slowly walked a few feet around to the other side of the rock pile, heart beating ever faster. Would an adult suddenly streak out of the rocks as I approached?

Then I found what I wanted, a wolf-sized hole under a rock, with a smooth floor right down to the permafrost. Pup scats lay just outside the entrance, and several more old bones littered the surroundings. I quickly retreated one hundred feet up a hill to another ridge and hid behind it. I was somewhat disappointed at seeing no wolves at the den, for I had expected the rest of the pack, or at least Mom, to be there. Still, she might be inside with the pups. Glad I had scared no one, I was somewhat unsettled that I still had no positive proof the den was occupied.

Hiding behind a rock and peering down at the den entrance, I began whining, thinking I could lure out Mom or one of the pups. Nothing. More whines, more nothing. I waited several minutes. Something seemed wrong. Reluctantly I decided to howl from behind the ridge. Surely that would bring out someone. I howled softly a couple of times and watched. Nothing again. Maybe the pups were still so small that they rarely came to the entrance, and perhaps Mom wasn't home.

All I could do at that point was to leave well enough alone. It was already almost midnight, so I decided to head out and return the next day to a hill about two hundred yards away. From there I could watch the den and see several miles in the direction the wolves usually seemed to travel.

TRIUMPH

I arrived at the hill about 10:00 A.M. It was a cold, blustery day, with intermittent rain and snow. Even with my down windsuit and arctic clothing, I periodically had to rise and pace around the hillside just to generate heat. All day I kept my vigil near the den, however, scanning all the surroundings with my binocs. Having spent years wanting to find a den like this, and knowing how close I was now, I found a few more hours of waiting painless.

Finally about 8:00 P.M. it paid off. A mile away a white speck was making its way toward the den. The speck was not a hare; it was a wolf! The animal quickly grew larger in my binoculars, and in no time it came to within a couple hundred yards of the den. But that was as close as it got.

Instead of coming west up the hillside to the den, the wolf remained in a north-south valley and continued north. My feelings were mixed. Maybe I hadn't found the den. Maybe this was the natal den where the pups had been born, but perhaps they had already been moved, as wolves often do. Whatever the case, here was a wolf that surely would lead me to the pups. They could not be far!

The wolf disappeared from my vantage point, so I quickly ran down my hillside and up the opposite to the next ridge. But I could not find the wolf. I ran down over the hummocks and back up to my trike. The going was too rough the way I had tried on foot, so I had to head around a different route. But finally I emerged back on top of the next ridge. I then zoomed northward another quarter mile, stopping intermittently and watching for wolves.

Then I saw them. The returning wolf was just meeting two others, two to three hundred yards from me, and they were all nosing each other and wagging tails in greeting. That was it! Now I was really excited. I knew I had to be near the den.

One of the wolves spotted me and came right over just as the others disappeared behind a rock pile at the top of a ridge. The wolf had a grayish back and sides, which in retrospect made it either one of the adult females or the yearling I came to know as "Scruffy." It circled me within twenty-five feet and appeared curious but unafraid. Again, I tossed it a few food bits, and it indulged. I was accepted even here, so close to the den!

We were situated at the brink of a valley running east and west and I was facing northward. Off to my right I could see the entire valley. The hillside ahead of me fell off steeply, thus obscuring the stream at the bottom. The hill opposite the valley facing me was bisected by a northward-running draw, down which a tiny stream flowed. I decided to wait where I was, let my newfound friend tire of me and leave, and then see where it went. If it headed toward where the other two wolves had disappeared, and did not reappear in any of the areas within my view in five minutes, I would assume the den was over the edge of the hill I was on.

By now I was experiencing a "runner's high" without running. I knew I was on the verge. My wolf finally left and dropped northward over the hillside. As the minutes passed and I did not see the animal reappear across the valley or off to my right, I took one more look around the horizon.

To my right and somewhat behind me, perhaps

Rock piles provide the ideal spot for wolf pups to hang out on the High Arctic tundra.

fifty miles away, was a row of snow-capped peaks. Straight to my right, a long mountain ten miles away extended for many miles north and south. Mind-boggling expanses of barren wilderness stretched in all directions. I tried to imagine what lay below me. A long rocky outcrop running northward formed the crest of a low ridge about fifty feet to my right. Perhaps an extension of it that I could not yet see sheltered the pups.

Five minutes was up. The wolf had not reappeared. I dismounted from the trike, heart pounding, and s-l-o-w-l-y a-n-d c-a-u-t-i-o-u-s-l-y started over the brink of the hill. This had to be it. I paralleled the rocky outcrop about fifty feet to the west. I could see now that the outcrop formed a cliff some twenty feet high as the huge rock slabs continued level, while the hill dipped to the valley. Cracks and crevices split the side of the ragged cliff both horizontally and vertically. Topping it all off at the end was a huge, weathered monolith, with an undercut face of lighter igneous webbing protruding through the darker beige sandstone. At the base, a series of shadowed entrances to what had to be a labyrinthine cave looked out to a view stretching for hundreds of square miles below. The perfect wolf den!

Suddenly a tall, all-white wolf emerged from around the east side of the outcrop and bounded up the hill between me and the den. A grayer, younger animal awoke from below the base of the outcrop, barked a couple of times and rushed toward me. Instantly wolves began running all around me, curious, cautious, alarmed, and upset. I didn't need to see the pups this time; I had definitely arrived!

But now what? I would have to try to get the pack used to me in this new and very sensitive situation. If it worked, I would be able to observe them close up in a way that had never been done before. However, the key to success would be to proceed slowly and cautiously. Overstepping my bounds just once might cause the wolves to keep the pups inside the den each time I appeared and possibly impart to them a fear of me that I could never overcome.

I realized that I must retreat and plan how to proceed. A tall, stark-white, smooth-furred wolf I later learned was the alpha male, or pack leader, rushed around intently with raised mane, barking coarsely at me as if to confirm my decision. It was clear I had already upset the pack, so I now had to control the damage and hope it had not been too much. As I hastily climbed back up the hill, the wolves swarmed around me some thirty to fifty feet away. I was exuberant!

Flushed with success and excitement, I thought of the tremendous potential this discovery held. I might finally be able to witness close up the interactions between adults and pups in a natural setting, and to discern the nature of the personal relationships among the adult members of the pack and among the pups. How and when does the pack decide to go hunting? Who stays home? How is the decision made? Precisely how are the pups fed? Are all pack members equally successful at food-getting? Do they all feed the pups? How does the leader of the pack relate to the others? What else might I learn that I could not even anticipate?

The questions came readily because of the many years I had been curious about wolves and the amount of experience I had studying them. I'd trapped and radio-tagged hundreds of wolves and observed them from the air since 1968. I'd maintained a captive colony of about thirty wolves for ten years and studied their behavior and physiology. I'd even raised wolves as pets. However, never had I, nor had anyone else, had the opportunity to actually live with a wild pack and get a subjective feel of its functioning. Now, on a busman's holiday, I might be on the verge of such an opportunity. I'd better not blow it.

I decided to leave the area completely and let the disturbance die down. The wolves seemed content to escort me to the top of the hill and watch as I disappeared over another. I slept little that night, knowing the situation's potential.

The next day I approached the den from the opposite direction. Fortunately I was decked in full winter garb. The polar wind that is one's almost constant companion here reminded me of the near-blizzard it had brought two days before. Winter snow patches still nestled in valleys and low spots. I carefully picked my way toward the crest of a broad open hillside that faced the rocky outcrop above and about two hundred yards across from it. Lying prone on a foam pad and pulling it with me as I inched to the crest, I could hardly contain myself until I peeked over the top.

One, two, three, four, five, six little beige bundles, along with all seven sprawled-out adults,

A pup rests below the ancient monolith that shelters its den.

Pack members approached the author, whom they already knew.

punctuated the dark green tundra hummocks lying just east of the den rocks. The wolves had not abandoned the den! Moreover, they were readily visible from my vantage point, so even if they did not accept me close to the den, at least I would be able to watch them from afar. The wolves were doing what I later learned they probably do best, or at least most—sleeping. But about an hour later, they awoke, and suddenly all thirteen were running, chasing, playing, and wagging tails. It was a glorious sight!

The whole pack soon made their way downhill and drank from a small stream running perpendicular to the lay of the rock outcrop, coming about fifty yards closer to me. The pups were light grayish brown with fuzzy fur, pointed ears, thin tails, and noses just starting to elongate and point. The little fuzzballs appeared to weigh five to ten pounds, and I judged them to be about five weeks old. But they seemed very vigorous. After about half an hour, six of the adults struck out up a valley west of me directly opposite the den and about a hundred yards to my right, but out of my view.

I stayed on my foam pad, peering at the pups, while the one remaining adult nosed around below. I recognized her as the mother of the pups, based on her conspicuous nipples, which I had seen earlier. Then she decided to take the pups for a walk in the same general direction the other adults had gone, except more to the east—right up toward me. There was no chance for me to retreat without being seen, so I just lay as still as possible. When the little caravan came to within about thirty yards, the adult suddenly grew very alert and excited. I then realized that the rest of the pack had come up behind me to within about fifty feet.

I was really embarrassed at having been caught so blatantly and having no direction in which to retreat without making matters worse. Thus I lay as still as I could while the female hurriedly led her pups back down the hill. Suddenly a gust of wind whisked my furry hat off and it blew along the ground. The scruffy wolf that had approached me the day before dashed over, grabbed my hat, and trotted off with it, followed by several others.

When I looked for the female and pups, I found that she had not taken them back to the den. Instead, to my great dismay, she had led them across the open hillside east of the den and way beyond. Thinking I had really fouled things up, I decided the best thing I could do was leave immediately. I stood up, picked up my gear, and headed in the opposite direction from the den.

The wolves began escorting me again, having dropped my hat, but I noticed that one had left and was catching up with the female and pups. As I ambled slowly away, disheartened, I saw that the two adults were now leading the pups in a circle back toward the den. Had the second wolf decided I was no threat and urged the female to return?

As I got farther away, the adults around me fell behind and eventually headed back toward the den. I waited about fifteen minutes and then returned to my vantage point. I then saw that the entire pack was back at the den sleeping. Maybe my presence wasn't so traumatic after all. I continued to watch.

Twice more in the next few hours, the main pack came to check me out, one venturing to within ten feet, and once the female and pups joined them. When she saw me, she again led the pups from the den, but this time the whole pack intervened when she was about an eighth mile away, and they all returned once more to the den and went to sleep. Finally, most of the pack came back up to within a few yards and gave me one final check. I lay as still as possible as they walked around me and went behind. I dared not turn around to see where they were or what they were doing, for fear of scaring them.

When I did finally turn around ten minutes later, I found that the pack had gone on hunting and were nowhere to be seen. The female and the yearling remained with the pups. During the next few hours, the two adults approached me five times and then returned to the den and pups. Finally, I retrieved my hat and headed back to camp to await arrival of the photographer. Again, it appeared the pack had accepted me in this new situation.

Returning the second day after finding the den, the author peered over a ridgetop and watched the entire pack head down a valley for a drink.

After the pack discovered the author spying on them, they approached to within 10 feet, and when a gust blew off the author's hat, Scruffy made off with it.

As is often the case elsewhere, the pack moved to a second den when the pups were about five weeks old.

SECOND THOUGHTS

"You'll never believe it," I blurted to the photographer as he stepped from the huge, roaring twin-otter aircraft.

"Did you find the wolves?" he asked.

"Den . . . pups . . . ten feet away . . . incredible . . . chance of a lifetime . . . unbelievable opportunity," I babbled, trying to relate the whole story in an instant to the only other person around who could fully appreciate what had transpired. I knew that Jim was just as obsessed with trying to photograph wolves as I was with studying them. Over a period of fifteen years I had tried numerous times to point him to opportunities to photograph wolves.

When I did finally get my whole story out, I don't think he really believed me. No doubt he accepted that I had found the den and seen the pups. But I think he suspected I may have exaggerated the ease of working with the pack.

Whatever the case, he eagerly joined me in returning to the den. As we approached, we caught sight of the pack in the distance in the midst of a major move from one den to another about an eighth mile away. It was quite a sight, with the whole line of seven adults and six pups strung out over the tundra, filing to their new quarters. The pups must have traveled twice the distance the adults did, for they had to climb over each hummock along the way.

At one point, the adults detected us, left the pups, and trotted over to within a hundred feet of us. They did not appear upset; the photographer was amazed. After about twenty minutes, the wolves returned to the pups and continued to the new den, a long series of rock piles with caves underneath. We were anxious to start photographing the pups, but since it was a clear afternoon and we had unlimited light ahead of us, we decided to play it cautiously. Thus we waited about three hours before making our way toward the new den.

As we approached, we saw no wolves. Carefully we moved closer. Suddenly my partner motioned ahead of us. To our great amazement, only about eighty feet ahead was a large furry pile of snoozing pups, the same color as the rocks and powdery soil surrounding them—but no adults. We both realized without question that we had been accepted. The pack was so indifferent to us that they had left their pups outside the new den with not a single adult to guard them, even though they knew we were nearby.

To facilitate our investigation, we decided to actually live with the wolves. We moved our tent to within a few hundred yards of the den and spent as much time with the pack as we could. This did pose some interesting logistical problems. We had little trouble keeping the animals out of camp when we were there. All we had to do was bark, and that discouraged them. However, when we were at the den, and the wolves passed our tent on their way to a hunt, they did cause problems.

We had to cache all our food in a rock pile far from the tent. Then we built several tall rock cairns about twenty feet away from the tent and fastened plastic streamers to their tops in hopes they might blow in the breeze and ward off the wolves when we were gone. Our precaution did little good, at least for

The second den was also a series of rock caves, which the pups darted in and out of.

The pack turns the tables and spies on the author's abode. The rock cairns, intended to deter the wolves, were more often used as scent posts.

At three to four weeks old, the wolf pups' ears, nose, and legs are short.

By five to six weeks of age, ears, nose, and legs have elongated.

us—the wolves found the cairns of considerable value. They peed on them regularly. Once they strewed our toilet paper all over the tundra. Another time they chewed the side out of my backpack.

The time that caused me the most consternation, however, came when from the den I spotted four of the wolves huddled excitedly all around the back of our tent. One wolf was forcing his nose through the drawstring-tightened porthole right behind the spot where I usually slept. For a few seconds the whole group waited with much suspense when the animal's head disappeared into the tent. Then, after a moment of great anticipation, the back of the wolf's head showed up again tugging and yanking, while his associates watched intently. Suddenly my red sleeping bag appeared, and the pack grew excited. They were eviscerating our tent, just like they pull the guts out of a musk ox!

Not wanting to frighten the pups or two adults with me at the den, I did not bark. Instead I cupped my hands and let out the sharpest, loudest high-pitched hoot I could muster. Instantly, the highly tensed wolves sprang away from the tent. Fleeing wildly, they rushed headlong for three hundred yards before stopping.

I was observing many new and interesting behaviors and making a good start at answering so many of the questions I had wondered about. I knew that my associates and I would find more answers—and new questions—on each trip as we studied the pack far into the future. But a serious qualm began to nag at me. Both the photographer and I had now realized a lifetime dream. We were bound to tell the world about it, not just because of our tremendous elation but also because we were working for *National Geographic*. Once the word was out, would media floodgates open? I knew that every outdoor magazine and TV nature series was interested in wolves, and I knew better than anyone how difficult the animals were to work with ordinarily.

I also realized that if anyone else were to attempt what I was doing, they could blow the whole effort and ruin the scientific research I needed to do. There were reasons why this had never been done before. A false move with these wolves, one wrong decision, one misstep, and the pack might be wary forever. We ourselves planned every move, took one step at a time, and constantly used our knowledge of wolves to help us remain in good standing with the pack.

Now that we were developing an article for publication, it seemed like the only way we could prevent a TV series from trying to follow up with their story was to do such a program ourselves. This, of course, would also bring further exposure, and would further jeopardize the situation.

Possibly it could jeopardize the wolves themselves. I could think of several reasons why that was highly unlikely. This area is much farther north than most hunters venture and is extremely difficult and expensive to get to. Access is carefully monitored by government personnel. We were allowed to go there because I was a scientist and we were working for *National Geographic*. I was granted a permit from the government to study and photograph the wolves, but the permit process was lengthy and involved. Still, ill thoughts about the situation continued to haunt me.

The pack pauses on its travels and sniffs the route ahead.

Mom, the mother of the pups, was one of the tamest of the pack.

THE FAMILY

I soon learned to identify each adult pack member individually close up, and I had sexed them by their urination postures. The adult males were tall and all white and had already shed; each bore, to various degrees, a dirty "mask," whose origin remained a mystery for over a year. The females were shorter legged and light greyish, with the rear half of their backs darker than the front half, and they shed for most of the summer. In my daily field notes, I named each individual.

Mom. Apparently the mother of the pups, this female spent the most time at the den with the pups. She was the thinnest of the adults and was constantly looking for something to eat. My impression was that she sacrificed considerably for her pups, never really getting much of a meal for herself, at least during July while we were there. Although I'd see her dig up and eat tidbits from caches around the den, she often would then regurgitate to the pups within the next half hour. Mom also seemed a bit paranoid, frequently ducking her head and looking up; perhaps she had been dive-bombed too many times by the long-tailed jaegers that pestered all the wolves. These predatory seabirds nest on the tundra and must constantly harass foxes and wolves to keep them from the nests.

In one way Mom was somewhat of an enigma. She clearly was not the top-ranking, or "alpha," female, as I had thought, but rather was middle-ranking, below Mid-Back and above Shaggy. Thus it was hard for me to understand how she could have been the mother of the pups, since it is usually the top-ranking female that produces pups. That is what dominance is supposed to be all about—jockeying for breeding rights.

Mid-Back. This female wolf, named for the prominent dark streaks starting behind her mane and covering the hindmost part of her back, was the most aloof wolf toward us. She tended to hang farther away from us than the rest of the pack and now and then would bark softly when we pointed the cameras at her. She was the most dominant, or alpha, female and she was a specialist at hunting arctic hares, frequently bringing them back to the den.

Shaggy. Shaggy seemed to be shedding the most, hence her name. Her dark back streaks were not quite as prominent as Mid-Back's, although from a distance one could be mistaken for the other. Shaggy was a shy wolf, probably because of all the females she was the most subordinate.

Alpha Male. Alpha Male was the most self-assured, confident-acting member of the pack, and the only one to lift his leg when urinating. He often had a dark-stained nose and a dirty smudge mark on his fur here and there. While not as friendly and unafraid as Scruffy, Alpha Male often approached us closely in a bolder sort of manner than the others. His stares were diffident and almost cautioning, and he was the undisputed master of the pack, at least during summer and probably year-around.

Alpha Male regularly dominated the other wolves, holding tail and ears up, standing stiff-legged, and growling, and they readily deferred to him. He also paid the pups the most attention of any of the males and acted like they were his, which they no doubt were. Once when Jim approached the pups too closely, about one hundred feet across the valley from their first den, old "Number 1" trotted over to them and swung his head to the side several times, pointing emphatically backward with his

Dark fur in the middle of this top-ranking female's back gave rise to her name, Mid-Back.

The lowest-ranking adult female was Shaggy, named for the fur hanging from her belly.

Alpha Male was pack leader, and all other wolves deferred to him. His raised mane and intent stare emphasized his impatience with lesser individuals, including the author.

Left Shoulder was an adult male with a fist-sized open wound behind his left shoulder, marking him distinctively.

53

nose, and the pups quite obediently all headed back to the den.

Motioning with the head, and actually bunting the pups with the nose, seems to be a common way in which the adults control where they want the pups to go. I was watching a lone pup playing around the stream once just below the den when Mid-Back came down and put her nose against the pup's butt and nudged the critter for fifty feet back up to the den.

Left Shoulder. Named for a fist-sized open wound just behind his left shoulder, this large male was second in command. He often tended to the pups, chewed bones with them, and patronized them, but not as much as Alpha Male. He seemed more mellow than Alpha Male, probably befitting his rank as the "beta" male. Left Shoulder was almost as tolerant of us as Alpha Male.

Lone Ranger. Lone Ranger looked much like the other two adult males, except that his facial mask was usually more apparent. He was a solid member of the pack but was the most aloof male, both to us and to the rest of the pack.

Scruffy. This was probably a yearling male, as indicated by his half-squat urination posture, with urine squirting from his mid-belly area. Unlike all the other males, Scruffy was gray, much like the females, although he stood taller than they. Scruffy followed us around regularly and sometimes lay down within a few feet of us when resting. He seemed curious, restless, reckless, and naive, and he possessed a streak of clownishness that certainly enlivened everybody's business. I once saw Scruffy awaken while all his packmates were asleep, wander over to an old dead arctic fox that had been a favorite toy of the pack for the past day, and deliver it to the pups. When they started killing it again for the hundredth time, he strolled back to his bed and went back to sleep.

Chances are good that Alpha Male was the father of the pups, so he would have a strong genetic stake in protecting them. Generally the males and females in a pack each form a dominance hierarchy, or social ladder, and usually it is the higher-ranking animals that breed. Even if the pups were not the pack leader's, they would almost certainly share some of his genes because usually most members of a wolf pack are related. The basic pack structure is much like that of a human family: Two unrelated, distantly related, or possibly closely related wolves mate and produce offspring each year. Some of the offspring may stay with the pack for up to four years, and possibly longer.

This explains why I observed so much cooperation in the care, feeding, and rearing of the pups. It was truly a communal effort. In fact, the pups were the center of the pack's universe. The only reason the adults returned to the den each day was to tend the pups. Wolves do not use dens for any other reason. If a pack fails to produce pups, or the pups are lost, the pack resumes its usual nomadic movement pattern within its territory. They ignore the den.

Lone Ranger sported a dark mask, later found to result from sticking his nose into the viscera of musk oxen while feeding. The author believes that the stain comes from the ox's gut contents.

The yearling male Scruffy was a clownish sort of wolf, with the size of an adult and the playfulness of a pup.

AT HOME WITH
THE ARCTIC WOLF

I had little idea how large the pack's territory was. However, in Alaska, where there is much more prey, wolf packs may range over a thousand square miles or more, a radius of more than eighteen miles. I once found my wolves fifteen miles from their den, returning from a musk ox herd another two miles away, so probably their territory covered at least a thousand square miles. It takes that much country to support enough vulnerable prey—musk oxen and arctic hares primarily, but also Peary caribou, ptarmigan, lemmings, seals, and miscellaneous nesting birds.

Feeding six rapidly growing pups is a strenuous job, and the pack devoted considerable time and effort to the task. Part of the pack's basic schedule was to strike out each day on the hunt from about 3:30 to 10:00 P.M. on clear days, or 2:00 to 11:00 A.M. on overcast ones. My impression is that it was usually the pups, Scruffy, or Mom that aroused the rest of the pack from their half-day-long sleeps and urged them on.

July 23 was typical. About 2:40 A.M., when the whole pack was sprawled on a heathery hillside just east of the den ridge, Mom arose and strolled to each of the adults, nosing the males perfunctorily but fully arousing Mid-Back. After Mid-Back stood reluctantly for a minute or two, she settled back down. Mom headed northeast about one hundred feet, looked back at the immobile adults, sat, threw her head back, and began howling, faintly at first but eventually stimulating the pups.

No one could sleep through the resulting aural exuberance from the pack's peanut gallery. Six strained, intertwining strands of soprano yowling

seemed to emphasize Mom's message: "We're hungry!" All the remaining pack members promptly joined the chorus, and the pups rushed them excitedly. Mom returned to the group, and the adults stiffly arose, stretched, socialized momentarily, and then followed Mom as she pranced off to the northeast on the nightly hunt.

On the other hand, most often Mom and/or Scruffy returned to the pups after a half hour and remained with them. Now I wish I had followed the pack several times to see at what point these animals broke away and returned. What were the circumstances? Did these babysitters decide on their own to return, or was it a group decision? Was there any coercion? Did Alpha Male play a role? Such questions remain to be answered, along with many others.

Take chorus howling, for instance. What is its role in the pack's social dynamics? One of my graduate students, Fred Harrington, and I studied howling in the Minnesota wolves and learned many of its functions. Fred recorded and analyzed hundreds of howls from my radioed wolf packs. Nevertheless, we still know no more about its role within the pack than when Lois Crisler wrote in *Arctic Wild* about the tame wolves she took to the Arctic and lived with: "Like a community sing, a howl is . . . a happy social occasion. Wolves love a howl."

I think we can eventually unravel the mystery of chorus howling with the High Arctic pack because it is so easy to observe the animals while recording their howling. And I have made a start. During 1986 alone, I noted group howling seventeen times. To

The pups use their den for shelter and security during their first eight weeks of life.

The commonest behavior of the wolf pack was to sleep, sometimes as long as nine hours.

generalize so far, the pack seems to howl on the following occasions: (1) when disturbed but not upset enough to flee, (2) when arising, (3) after intense playing or social interactions, and (4) when split up. The only common denominator among these situations seems to be arousal. But why must wolves howl when aroused?

Whatever the reason, pups pick up the trait early. Our pups howled the first day I found them, when about five weeks old. Certainly they could use howling to get attention, and I once saw a pup that had fallen a quarter mile behind the others return to the pack after a great deal of howling by the pup and the pack. Nevertheless, on another occasion, when a lone pup strayed a quarter mile from the den, Mom merely tracked it down and escorted it back without any vocalization.

Such observations are exactly the kind I had hoped to make when I first discovered the den, and I made far more than I ever anticipated. Some of the information I obtained was mundane. For example, the basic pack routine was sleep, bouts of play and social interaction lasting up to two hours, a daily

hunt by most of the adults, and feeding of the pups whenever possible.

I never ceased to wonder about the amount and intensity of the pup's play. One day when about seven weeks old, the pups moved to an old snowfield about one hundred feet across in a depression on a hillside about a quarter mile up a valley from the den. For about forty-five minutes the pups scrambled back and forth across the snowfield, chasing one another, tackling, sliding, rolling, skidding, and carrying on to a degree I have never seen nor heard of before for any species. Sometimes they would pair up and wrestle like three tag teams on a snowy mat, and now and then Scruffy, who was really only an adult-sized pup himself, would rush in and attack the whole batch. Once he playfully grabbed one pup by the nape and hoisted its front quarters right off the snow.

Along with the intensive play, an occasional excursion, and the long hours of sleep, the pups' only other major activity was eating. They did that with great gusto as well. In fact, their basic feeding routine demanded gusto. To obtain most of their food,

58

Time to get up. The adults stretched frequently, especially on awakening.

The pack engaged in group howling during times of high arousal: on awakening, during intense social interaction, and sometimes when individuals, especially pups, were separated from the pack.

wolf pups must go through an elaborate ritual. As an adult approaches, especially one just returning after a long absence, the pups race each other to the animal, whining and wagging the entire rear halves of their bodies as they approach. When they meet the adult, they crouch and wag excitedly, hold their ears back, and lick rapidly at the mouth of the adult. Each competes frantically with the others in mobbing the adult and trying to get closest to the animal's mouth.

Usually the adult accepts the feverish solicitations for a few seconds, turns, and rushes away excitedly, weaving body and tail from side to side. The adult holds its head low, and the pups follow and try to continue mobbing its mouth. The adult may travel only a few feet or sometimes up to a quarter mile before stopping and suddenly regurgitating. The pups then frantically gobble up every bit of food that falls. Within less than thirty seconds, nothing is left. He or she who hesitates is truly lost.

This food-transfer process helps select for pups that are aggressive and large, and it increases any differences among pups: The rich get richer, the

poor get poorer. This explains why in Minnesota I sometimes find litters in which some pups weigh twice as much as others.

The adult does not necessarily empty its stomach each time it feeds the pups, for during the next few hours, it may regurgitate two or three, or possibly more, times. Most often it was Mom or Scruffy who fed the pups, probably because these two spent the most time around the den where they could dig up food cached by the rest of the pack, and of course they were hounded the most by the pups. Nevertheless, I saw each of the other pack members, except Lone Ranger, regurgitate to the pups.

Although the main function of food begging and regurgitating is clearly to deliver food to the pups, there may be more to this interesting behavior than immediately apparent. I often saw adults competing with pups for food scraps lying around the den, yet after an adult succeeded in gobbling up the food, it would eventually regurgitate to the pups. Because pups also devour pieces of prey brought to them directly, it is clear they do not need predigested food, so that does not seem to explain this behavior.

The pups often played around a snowfield, with much chasing and running back and forth on and near it.

One possibility is that regurgitating food allows an adult to control when it grants the food to the pups, and asserting such control seems to be an important need. For example, I once watched Alpha Male regurgitate to two pups. One immediately made off with a large chunk, while the other fed on the remaining pieces. The adult then growled at the pup and began re-eating the regurgitant. If he was training the pup to be competitive, it worked, for the pup quickly grabbed a chunk and fled with it.

On another occasion, Mid-Back, the pack's specialist in hare hunting, returned excitedly to the den area with a whole hare in her mouth. She strode rapidly by the other pack members, tail raised and hackles up. Scruffy ran to meet Mid-Back and escorted her solicitously as she headed to a favorite resting spot below the den itself, lay down, and proceeded to flagrantly devour her catch. Scruffy lay beside her, groveled several times, and pawed fetchingly at her, and finally, just as the last stiff, furry hind foot was moving down Mid-Back's throat, he maneuvered directly in front of Mid-Back's head and slid his nose right up to the hare's foot in one

last, desperate beg. The foot disappeared down Mid-Back's throat.

Question: Why didn't Mid-Back simply consume the hare where she had caught it and avoid all Scruffy's begging? Why deliver it to the den area with such flourish? Is there prestige, status, or some other social intangible to be gained by displaying one's catch? by regurgitating to the pups?

Certainly with food being so difficult to obtain, it might play an important role in pack relations, and social relations are extremely important to a wolf pack. They are the currency of the dominance hierarchy, which in turn sets the social structure of the pack, with top-ranking males and females, subordinates, and even "scape-wolves."

Other than the pack leader's position, which itself was not all that obvious, the other wolves' ranks on the social ladder took much watching for me to discern. The mother of the pups should have been a high-ranking wolf, but Mom often seemed to be the most submissive member of the pack, except perhaps for Scruffy. Among the adult males, there were few dominance interactions, and none of these

Feathers and bones became handy props as the pups played around the den.

The pups rest and sleep most of the time, interspersed with short bursts of feeding and playing.

When an adult returned to the den, it would lead the pups away to feed them.

After taking the pups a distance away, from a few yards to as much as a quarter mile, the adult would regurgitate food to them, and instantly they would gobble it up.

Scruffy returns to the pack with a young artic hare.

animals was clearly Mom's mate.

Finally the answer dawned on me, or so I thought. No one has really had the chance to observe such interactions so close up before with a wild pack. Our present model for wolf social interactions is based primarily on captivity studies during the courtship and breeding season. What observations there have been of wild packs have been cursory, and most were made in winter. But this was midsummer. That is when the wolf's reproductive hormones are at their annual low. In short, it is a period of relative social peace. It might also be the time for an annual social reshuffle to begin. I was observing this social flux. The real contests, and those among the males, would not get underway until winter.

Possibly Mom had been the top female last year, so she got bred. However, as she devoted her energies and most of her food to the pups, she grew thinner and thinner. Such sacrifice would pay off for her genetically, for she would have six strong, healthy offspring to pass on her genes.

The only exception to the relative lack of domi-

nance demonstrations I observed involved the pups. The adults were always "pinning" the pups, that is, forcing them to lie still with their necks to the ground. Why? Probably to constantly suppress the pervasive expansion tendency each wolf seems to be born with. It certainly was clear when the pups were away from the adults that each thought it could take over the world. Such an outlook would eventually be valuable when as an adult a wolf would have to routinely dart in and out among the thrashing hooves of a swirling herd of musk oxen. However, until such time, it would facilitate the pack's life if the pups just let the adults handle the important things.

The pups were constantly pinning each other, too. Play fighting allows each pup to test and hone its competitive skills, and this is extremely important. Although pack functioning appears to be a model of cooperation, especially during the peaceful summer period, the basic selfish, competitive spirit of every living thing lurks constantly beneath. Nowhere was this more apparent than after the wolves made a kill.

Mid-Back specialized in hunting arctic hares. Usually she consumed the front quarters first.

Pups play-fight regularly, probably testing their social rank as they grow and change.

The entire hare is eaten, including fur and viscera. Even the hind foot — really only fur and bone — is downed.

THE GREAT MUSK OX HUNT

From any high spot on the barren grounds I could scan hundreds of square miles. Musk oxen are dark and artic hares white, and both usually travel in herds. Thus I was able to watch the wolves hunt both hares and musk oxen.

The most outstanding hare hunt I saw was very nonconventional. During early morning on July 25, I was making my usual nightly vigil from the hill immediately above and south of the den. I could see most of the wolves flopped out in the heather 150 feet downhill to the northeast. I could also view the activity area below, just west of the den, where a few hours before, I had watched Mid-Back tormenting Scruffy by devouring the hare before his very eyes. Across the valley to my left, a huge hill loomed a quarter mile away, covered on its side by the usual hummocks but smooth with gravel on top. It was just about 4:00 A.M., and the wolves had been flat since 1:30. My only excitement had come from swatting mosquitoes, which had discovered that since the previous day's snow had stopped, they could pester me without dodging snowflakes.

At 4:09 A.M., Mom suddenly looked up from her long snooze and stared momentarily at a white form a quarter mile away atop the big hill across the valley. She arose and trotted down the valley and up the hill straight toward what must be an adult hare. But surely the wolf didn't think she could ever catch the hare. It had all the advantages, being on top of the hill and able to intently watch the wolf approaching. Still the hare stuck tight as Mom labored over the hummocks and up the hill. Finally, when the wolf was about fifty yards away, the hare headed out.

"I told you so," I thought.

Mom made a token dash, slowed, and then nosed around where the hare had been. Suddenly the ground burst in front of her, and two or three young, gravel-colored hares sprang away. The wolf instantly chose the one streaking straight down hill and nabbed it at the bottom. Had the wolf seen these invisible hares from a quarter mile away? Or had she suspected they were there from the behavior of the adult?

With musk oxen, of course, the wolf's problem is not to catch them but to kill one without getting damaged itself. Males may weigh a half ton or more, and females half that, and they live in herds of up to thirty. When defending calves, adults squeeze together in a tight line or semicircle in front of the calves or in a circle with the calves inside. They have been known to kill wolves.

The problem in attempting to observe such tactics and how wolves try to overcome them was to get close enough to both musk oxen and wolves at the same time. Because it was far more fruitful for me to watch at the den than to try to keep up with the wolves while they scampered over the hummocks and up and down the hills on a hunt, my hopes began to fade. Until July 15, that is.

We had been watching at the den since 10:30 A.M. and had noticed a herd of eleven adult and three calf musk oxen below us a mile and a half away, approaching gradually from the east. The herd picked its way up and down the uneven terrain, scrounging the grasses and sedges that form their main summer diet. At times the herd would disappear in a depres-

The pups, always begging for something to eat, no doubt help motivate the adults to venture out on a hunt.

69

sion, only to reappear in dark clumps here and there.

The wolves seemed pretty tired all day, and except for a short excursion with the pups 150 feet to the stream below and a play session there, little out of the ordinary happened. By 5:00 P.M., the musk oxen were only a mile away, so we busied ourselves observing them as well as the wolves, which were on the opposite side of the ridge we were watching from. Because the sky was perfectly clear, we expected the wolves to strike out on their hunt sometime in the evening.

"You know, Jim," I said, "if the wolves spot that herd and head down there, the whole thing might be over before we're packed up. What say we take a chance and get into position near the herd just in case?"

"Exactly what I've been thinking," the photographer replied. "The most we have to lose is a night's observation here, and we can make that up anytime."

It was one of our best decisions in this whole adventure. We immediately headed to the herd. The musk oxen were feeding and resting on a half-mile-wide plateau between two creeks. The terrain, while level, comprised hummocky polygon platforms some twenty to fifty feet wide, separated by troughs several feet across and a yard or so deep. Old bleached bones of a caribou and two disintegrating musk ox skulls perhaps hundreds of years old accented the sense of timelessness I felt in that proximity to the herd of shaggy beasts. Had I beamed back to the Stone Age?

Although we could glimpse wolves moving about on the den ridge a mile away, much of the route between the den and the musk oxen was obscured. However, soon after we positioned ourselves near the herd, some of the wolves seemed to be heading in our direction. Then they disappeared. About 7:30 P.M., all seven reappeared, threading their way diagonally down a hillside to our right; they had spotted the musk oxen! The wolves moved very deliberately, with little lingering, but at their usual five-mile-per-hour pace. They seemed interested but not too excited. Then I realized that this was nothing special for them. They see musk oxen every day.

But it certainly was special for me. I had observed only one other wolf encounter with musk oxen, just a week before, and it had been disappointing. The wolves had approached the herd and then lay down near it until distracted by a passing hare, which they spent the next half hour trying to catch. And that was it.

This time proved more exciting, although it started out basically the same as the other. The wolves approached the herd quite casually, and the musk oxen tightened and faced them. Each adult ox continually shifted its rear end around slightly, pressing against its neighbor. The wolves stood and watched ten feet away, with Scruffy hanging back a few feet. After several minutes, most wolves lay down, although now and then individuals got up and walked around. They did not seem excited.

The musk oxen, however, took the situation seriously. They stood facing their adversaries, heads lowered and calves huddled at their rumps. Nevertheless they appeared disorganized. Single oxen on the edges eventually broke rank, and some seemed more interested in eating. Neither did the wolves have it all together. At one point, Scruffy and one of the adult males started strolling away from the musk oxen while another adult male on the other side of the herd challenged the beasts.

As the casual confrontation continued, however, wolves prowling around behind the herd seemed to unnerve the musk oxen. Gradually the situation changed into one in which the oxen were more scattered, and the wolves walked about between subgroups. Every now and then a skirmish developed when an ox charged a wolf, even though other wolves and musk oxen just stood around nearby.

Such maneuvering and skirmishing interested the wolves more, and soon they became more active. The unevenness of the terrain may also have played a role, for when an ox ran, it had to maintain its footing while carrying its great weight on spindly legs in and out of the troughs without stumbling. Whatever the case, the pace increased, and wolves actually began chasing subgroups of musk oxen. As soon as they got close, the oxen would swing around, stand, and threaten. However, with seven wolves chasing various groups, and the groups trying to keep together, the entire herd began gyrating.

The wolves grew increasingly excited. Soon they started darting in and out among the frantic musk oxen, often passing within inches of them. The shaggy oxen would turn and charge with lowered heads, and strike out with front hoofs. Through our lenses, the scene grew surrealistic: big dark whirling beasts; long white streaks; clouds of dust; swerving, streaking, twisting, charging; black masses, white streaks, dust—the Stone Age!

Fourteen musk oxen and seven wolves, all in a swirling, chaotic, dusty mass. The noise, the dust, the motion, the frenzy, drew us straight into the fray. It grew hard to remain objective. Although I have watched wolf packs chasing moose, deer, and caribou, that was always from an airplane, where I was clearly a spectator. It was different here. We were almost in the middle of this primeval scene, especially since the wolves streaking among those massive oxen were not just wolves. They were Scruffy, Mom, Mid-Back, Alpha Male, Left Shoulder, Shaggy, and the Lone Ranger.

I was certain we would see one of our wolves killed or seriously hurt. The herd was reluctant to run far, so the attack turned into a localized harassment, back and forth on the flats, up and down through the troughs. The wolves clearly handled the terrain better. Once an ox even fell over and lay on its back with all four feet up in the air, and the wolves rushed in and nipped at it.

It's hard to say how long the skirmishing went on. We completely lost track of time, but it probably lasted an hour or more, and the pace kept increasing. Run, stand, run, stand, run, stand. Run, run, stand; run, run, stand; run, run, run, stand; run, run, run, run, run. The herd panicked.

"We're going to see a kill!" Jim shouted prophetically.

Thirty seconds later, Alpha Male and Mom closed in on a calf, and Mom grabbed it by the right side of its head. Alpha Male latched onto its nose. The rest of the pack quickly gravitated to the pair and their quarry, while the calf's mother joined the stampeding herd. As the calf struggled, it gradually dragged the six wolves stuck to its head and shoulders down a slope.

Then, suddenly, Left Shoulder, who had the most posterior grasp on the calf's right side, let up and rushed off after the herd, which, now in a complete rout, was fleeing down off the plateau into the creek bottom. Mid-Back, who had the last hold on the calf's other side, soon left to join him. They hit the second calf crossing the creek.

The herd turned to its right and rushed down the creekbed one hundred yards to a river. One big bull stopped and stood its ground. More wolves left the first calf, while Mom and Alpha Male held their grip. The calf was no longer on its feet, and soon the male left. Down in the creek, Left Shoulder and Mid-Back worked on the second calf, as their packmates joined them. And in the distance, the remaining twelve musk oxen, including a calf, were fleeing up the side of the huge bank toward another plateau. The calf and a couple of adults were far to the rear.

Then—I couldn't believe it—fifty yards behind the musk oxen, far away on the hillside, ran another wolf, either Shaggy or Mid-Back. She was after the third calf! The calf was running along the right side of an adult, and another adult was fifteen feet behind. The wolf caught up quickly, and just at the top of the hill, she grabbed the calf from the right. The adults continued to run, except for the two with the calf. But the closer one did not face the wolf, and the other had stopped partway up the hill. Alpha Male arrived and joined the female wolf. The calf continued to struggle and eventually dragged both wolves all the way back down the hill to the river. There they were joined by others, and the calf fell.

Still the job was not over. The frenzied wolves now became very intent and businesslike. No greetings, no socializing. They reminded me of firefighters springing to life to put out a fire. But the wolves' goal was to remove as much from the kills as they could as quickly as possible. It seemed now like each wolf considered the others competitors. Each would feed for twenty minutes to almost an hour, then sneak off furtively and regurgitate into a cache. Several interspersed this activity with wading into the river and drinking. Mom and Scruffy took loads up to the den right away, and others did later. Alpha Male remained near the kill for hours.

While I sat and watched the wolves at work close up, preparing to convert the recent calves to wolf pups, I realized what an extraordinarily rare observation I had made. It happens all the time in the High Artic, of course, but there's usually nobody around to watch.

As the wolves approach a herd of musk oxen, the burly beasts begin to move toward each other.

Temporarily stymied by the herd's defensive tactics, the wolves stop and look the situation over.

The herd presents a formidable front, with calves huddled behind.

As the wolves charge, the herd intensifies its defense.

The wolves' maneuverings unnerve the musk oxen, and this seems to encourage the wolves.

More skirmishing, and the herd begins to panic.

The wolves give chase.

Overleaf: After considerable give and take between wolves and musk oxen, the situation turns into a rout, and the wolves close in on a calf.

The usual points of attack on a musk ox calf are the nose, ears, and other parts of the head.

After a few minutes, the calf drops.

In attacking a second calf from the stampeding herd, a wolf darts in from the right and aims for the head.

A second wolf dashes in to assist.

The cow abandons the doomed calf.

After the struggle carries the wolves and calf down the hill, other pack members join in.

The wolves then begin to fill themselves so as to transport parts of their bonanza back to the pups.

First they open the calf at the abdomen.

Soon the animals start to eviscerate the calf.

Overleaf: The abdomen is opened widely, exposing all sorts of wolf goodies.

Through intense tugging, great chunks are torn from the carcass.

Large, loose pieces like this liver are ideal for taking away and caching.

After gorging, the wolves often wash up and drink in the nearest body of water.

Some wolves carry food back to the pups in their mouths.

A fellow biologist, Dr. David Gray, the ultimate authority on wolf and musk ox interactions, observed some twenty-one encounters between wolves and musk oxen on Bathurst Island over an eleven-year period. My observations parallel his, but his provide a better perspective. Of the twenty-one interactions Gray saw, involving from one to ten wolves and up to twenty-seven musk oxen per herd, only three led to kills. Clearly I had been very lucky to actually see three at once.

The scene I had just witnessed cannot be typical; otherwise there would be no calves left and thus no musk oxen. (Later I observed several more herds with calves in this pack's territory.) Conceivably our presence, or our machines, or our cameras or picture-taking could have affected the outcome of this interaction. I've sometimes wondered that about our aircraft when aerially observing wolves chasing prey.

Still, during all such interactions, both the predator and the prey seem so intent on the other that it appears they tune out peripheral activity. I've known very shy wolves, for example, to chase deer through someone's yard and kill it right there while everyone watched. As soon as they make such a kill and then realize how exposed they are, they flee, to return after dark and drag away the carcass.

We certainly cannot be sure of a lot of things. Science only progresses by multiple observations, repeated trials, cross-checking, challenges, and skepticism. Eventually we end up obtaining valid information. In this case, even if we had some unknown influence, I still got a magnificent glimpse into a hitherto elusive part of the wolves' and musk oxen's world. Later I would get even a closer look, and I hoped sometime in the future I would see enough such encounters to obtain a truly valid picture of their nature.

For now it is clear that, just with all the other wolf/prey interactions I have seen, there is generally a rough balance between the prey's defenses and the predator's abilities. That balance results in the threatening, the charging, the testing, the chasing, the harassing, the mixing and infighting, the feints, the attacks, and the counterattacks that transpire between wolves and prey. Gray observed one wolf attack that lasted 230 minutes, interspersed with the same kind of resting I had seen earlier. Excluding the intermissions during Gray's observation, the wolves and musk oxen actually mixed it up for two hours and forty-six minutes. That's indicative of a pretty good balance.

Within two days after I observed the calf kills, there wasn't a shred of bone or hair left at any of them. The pack had devoured or cached some three hundred pounds, and much of it was already converted to wolf pups. For days the wolves delivered food to the pups from the caches, and the pups grew and changed noticeably. The musk ox herd too was gone, having headed miles away to the vicinity of other groups, many of which still possessed their calves. Back at the wolf den, the adults rested a great deal, especially the day after the kill, and the next day they socialized more than we had ever seen before. It was like a great burden had been lifted, and now it was time for celebration.

For me it was time for philosophizing. Before this trip I had tried every method I could think of to observe, study, and photograph wolves, but I had caught only a few mere glimpses compared to the present bonanza. Not only was I actually living with a pack of wolves, but I had just shared an incredibly intense, intimate, and atavistic experience with them. For one who had spent most of his life seeking to know the wolf, this had truly been the ultimate trip.

I had videotaped the wolves during all of their activities except the musk ox chase. (My camcorder was out of order for a few weeks during that period.) I had recorded many precious moments during the life of the pack that would sustain me when I returned to civilization. Nevertheless, I dreaded leaving the pack. For much of the summer I had spent more time with the wolves than with people, and—I'll admit it—I had grown attached to them.

Thus on my last day with the pack in 1986, I hoped to take a few last scenes of each wolf. Some of them, especially Scruffy, I might never see again. I knew I would return in 1987, although I had no definite plan for how to obtain funding for the trip.

When I arrived at my lookout across from the wolves' current headquarters, a "rendezvous site" or temporary resting area a quarter mile west of the den, I found them all asleep. Rendezvous sites are like above-ground dens—areas where the pups stay while the adults are off hunting. Pups usually do not use dens after about eight weeks of age but rather spend their time resting, playing, and growing in

A six-to-seven-week-old pup surveys the scene around his den.

the rendezvous sites. The adults, then, always know where to return when heavily laden with food.

I was sorry at first that the wolves were so zonked out, for I wanted to say goodbye in some sort of way, perhaps by videotaping the pack as I actually left. I realized, of course, that such a gesture would have no meaning for them. They could not know that I was leaving for almost a year. Nor could they care. But a human wants to say goodbye when leaving friends.

Still, I was not about to wake them up. Instead, the scientist in me prevailed. I lifted the camcorder, recorded the whole pack peacefully asleep, took one long last look at Scruffy, Mom, and Alpha Male, Lone Ranger, Mid-Back, Shaggy, Left Shoulder, and their six pups, and the ancient pristine hills and valley that were their home. I then turned and headed away, shifting my mental gears to help prepare myself to resume my life as a human being. I did not look back.

Mom and a curious three-to-four-week-old pup sniff a tuft of fur.

RETURN TO THE FAMILY

When I returned to the High Arctic the next year, I could hardly contain myself. A million questions flashed through my mind, along with a certain amount of trepidation.

I had spent the intervening ten months thoroughly engrossed in the rest of my life: studying the wolves in the Superior National Forest of Minnesota and in Denali National Park in Alaska, while also advising on a planned red wolf reintroduction to North Carolina and on a study of natural recolonization of wolves to northwestern Montana. In addition I pursued such other time-consuming and intensive activities as trying to help establish an International Wolf Center in Ely, Minnesota, working on various writing projects, and discharging responsibilities for the Eastern Timber Wolf Recovery Team and the IUCN/SSC International Wolf Specialist Group.

Thus I had not really had much time to think about my High Arctic family. Furthermore, it was hard to imagine the pack for most of the year because they would be living in total darkness. By late September the constant light of summer has already flipflopped to winter's twenty-four hours of darkness. Because I had no idea what the wolves do during that time, where they travel, how they hunt, or when they are active, it was difficult to imagine them and what they might be doing in that bitter cold place for most of the year.

Both in my office and in my home several picture mosaics of the pack adorned my walls. There was Alpha Male, his mane raised and his eyes constantly glaring at me, Scruffy howling from on top of a rock, and of course Mom with pups swirling around her, and all the other pack members in various poses. One whole frame of twenty pictures recalled the great musk ox chase, during which the pack plundered the hapless herd of nomadic musk oxen passing through the area.

But the pictures were flat, and unless I took the time to immerse myself in recollections about the previous summer, there were too many other things to fill my mind. Thus the only time I really got into wondering about my pack was after giving a talk about them or discussing them with friends or acquaintances.

Now, however, all those other distractions were thousands of miles away. I could concentrate on my wolf pack.

And I had been speculating for several days, for that is how long it takes to get to the pack from Minnesota. Although the first part of the trip is by commercial aircraft, the last several hundred miles must be covered either by a charter flight or by hitchhiking a ride with other scientists passing through the area. There is much waiting around for just the right flight that might have room. During that time my patience is severely tested. I usually bring reading material and work to do, but being "so near and yet so far" becomes frustrating. I can almost taste my curiosity.

Eager beyond belief to see what kind of a greeting I would receive from my wolf pack, I headed directly to the den as soon as possible after landing on the island. As I covered the last half mile, the questions were overflowing. Who will be there? Will they remember me? How many pups will they have? Will they have any? Will they even be there? What about last year's pups? How will they respond? Will Scruffy be there? I wondered about each particular individual. There could be as many as thirteen wolves now, the seven adults from 1986 and their six pups. The 1986 pups would be grown up now and look like adults, although they might all act like Scruffy, last year's yearling.

I knew the wolves had to be at the den, unless some real tragedy had befallen them. Unlike in areas further south, this was the only possible den for at least several hundred square miles, so if the pack was going to have pups again, it had to be here. Still, way back in the deep recesses of my mind I knew that the logic of the statement "they've got to be there" was underlain with a desperate dose of fervent wishful thinking.

Nevertheless, the varied assortment of old prey bones, probably dating back hundreds of years, indicated that numerous generations of wolves had been raised here. I had once compared the bones with those at Fort Conger on northeastern Ellesmere Island, where Greely had first stayed over winter and Perry had later camped. The den bones looked older, which would make them at least one hundred years old. Could it be that wolves had denned here one hundred years ago or more? (I got my answer after submitting to a lab for radiocarbon dating a musk ox bone that I had dug up from around the den. The result: 233 years ± 70.)

As in 1986, I was alone when I first approached the den. This time I was the advance man for a television film crew. After agonizing for months over the decision, I had realized that no doubt someone would insist on producing a TV special about this remarkable pack and our relations with it. That "someone" might better be Jim and I, for we knew we could do it without disturbing the wolves. Then media interest would be depleted, and I could settle down and study this pack in earnest. The pack would be safe from everyone, for I would be living with them each year, complete with an exclusive government permit.

For now, it would be another summer gathering what scientific data I could but concentrating on filming and assisting with the TV production. We had made a deal with National Geographic Television and the BBC to produce the film. Thus I needed

to scout out the situation and make sure we actually had subjects and the subjects were still photographable. I also needed to film close-ups of the pups themselves and the mother nursing them, for at this age — about three weeks — the pups change daily. By the time my partners were supposed to arrive, the pups would be much larger and different looking. Also the mother might already have stopped nursing them, and it was critical to get nursing scenes.

As I reached the hill just south of the den, two adult wolves approached excitedly. One tall, white, friendly male strode right up, and I thought he might be Scruffy, the carefree, gray-backed yearling male of 1986, in a new adult coat and a more mature demeanor. The other, a shorter gray-backed female, was not so comfortable. Several times she barked and started to howl. The male walked over to an old musk ox skeleton, raised his leg and urinated on it, then defecated.

I was somewhat chagrined. The way each wolf approached, I knew they recognized me. But did I recognize them? Looking at each was like trying to pick out of a crowd an old friend after many years, years in which he may have lost his hair, grown a beard, and gained twenty pounds.

Suddenly a tiny dark pup emerged from the den area and headed toward the female. However, the little pup soon detected me and was afraid enough that it quickly returned to the den. Clearly I could not push things too fast or too far. My first need was to accustom the adults to me again.

Overall I was elated that the wolves remembered me and that they had pups. This certainly meant that I could make my observations, and that we could obtain the movie footage we needed for the documentary. However, from a personal standpoint, I was disturbed that I could not readily recognize these wolves.

In 1986 I had recorded any peculiarity of each individual adult, especially marks or mannerisms that might be long-lasting. However, to distinguish these individual characteristics, I usually had to see the wolf from all sides and watch it carefully, sometimes even comparing it with packmates to be sure. Thus on a day-to-day basis I had learned to recognize them primarily from temporary traits such as the shedding patterns, a fresh injury, or the current shape of the muzzle mask.

That muzzle mask had been a real puzzle to me in

Mom and pups close in for a look at the camera. Eventually one of the pups untied the author's bootlaces.

1986. Generally males tended to have it most distinctly, and over the weeks its shape would change. It was a dark stainlike smudge on one or both sides of the muzzle in front of the eyes and often bridging the nose. One possibility was that it was from soil, as if the wolf had stuck his muzzle into a lemming hole. The problem with this explanation was that I never saw them do such a thing. The only time I watched them hunt lemmings their behavior at the hole was to sniff at a tundra hummock excitedly and then dig at it, and it was the females that tended to do that. The correct explanation finally came later in 1987, in a way I could not have anticipated.

An additional factor that would confuse the situation this year was the change that young wolves undergo from one year to the next. The six pups from 1986, who would now be yearlings, would be totally unrecognizable except by elimination of the other adult pack members seen in 1986. In other words, if all the other pack members were accounted for, then any other wolf with them would almost certainly be one of the 1986 pups, especially if it also gave signs of being young: being especially shy or very friendly, being perhaps a bit smaller, having fuzzier fur, showing submissiveness, and so on.

Then there was Scruffy. Scruffy was a yearling male in 1986, as indicated by his urination posture, general submissive behavior to all the other adults, and particular interest in playing with the pups. Unlike the three adult males in the pack in 1986, Scruffy had a grayish back similar to that of the three adult females, although he was distinguishable from them by his lankier stance.

I thought that the reason Scruffy was colored more like the adult females was because he had not yet developed adult levels of male hormones. Thus, for example, young males tend to squat-urinate more like adult females rather than standing to void. When Scruffy was two years old, he probably would have an all-white coat like the adult males.

In addition to the possibility of Scruffy's coat color changing from 1986 to 1987, his personality probably would also have changed. He might be wary; he would probably be less playful and less curious. He might also be gone. The commonest age for wolves to disperse from the pack is as yearlings. Of all the 1986 pack members, the one I most expected to disperse was Scruffy.

Thus when I first approached the den again in 1987 and the two wolves came up to me I really didn't know what to think. The tall white one, which was very friendly, later proved to be Alpha Male. I still am not sure who the antsy female was.

I hung around within sight of the den and adults, reminding them that I meant no harm. Twice more I spied the pup. The adult male was totally at ease, and eventually the female calmed down. So as not to stretch my luck, I left after a few hours.

The next day was most heartening. A total of six adult-sized wolves approached me around the den, and I could count at least five pups, three to four weeks old. Although I recognized only Alpha Male and Mom, all the adults were unafraid. I suspected that several were yearlings, and as long as their parents accepted me, they too apparently realized I was OK.

This principle also seemed to apply to the pups. Last year, when we had first approached the pups, they were about five weeks old, and they remained warier of us than did the adults. These younger pups, however, were tamer.

Just how tame I would soon find out. Seeing that everyone was now so comfortable with me, I decided to start shooting as quickly as possible. I set up the movie camera and tripod about fifty feet from the den and aimed it toward the front, where it appeared that Mom usually nursed the pups. Soon Mom spotted me there and came over, two little pups atow. Mom needed to check me out, so she spent much time prowling around me and sniffing. One of the pups decided to be more direct. It waddled up and down over the hummocks, even tumbling into the troughs, till it reached my boot.

The tiny tyke was the cutest pup I had ever seen. Ears just starting to point, nose pugged, and legs still stubs, the little furball figured this new part of his world was well worth exploring. Not only was my boot toe smooth and rubbery, but some interesting long cords hung from the top. The pup had never experienced anything like this thing before. He bit the cords and started tugging on them. They gave. He pulled some more, and they gave some more. Within only a minute or two, the little pup had completely untied the bow of my boot lace!

Although there were a few times when yearlings returned without adults and barked and howled at me, finally they learned that I was acceptable. Eventually most of the yearlings dispersed, as I thought

During his second summer with the pack, the author first approached the den when the pups were only three to four weeks old and still nursing.

they would, and the pack totaled six adults and five pups. I finally recognized each of the adults from last year, except for Scruffy.

Later in 1987, after I had figured out who all of the regular six adults were, a seventh wolf showed up, looking a lot like Scruffy did in 1986, and just as friendly. The only problem was, when this one urinated it clearly was a female, her bottom almost touching the ground as she squatted. Although Scruffy had also squatted in 1986, his was only a half squat and the urine shot from his underside rather than from his bottom. Thus the seventh wolf in 1987 must have been one of the 1986 pups returning to the pack. That animal came and went several times as I watched the pack in August. It was the only yearling I saw at the den during that month.

A three-to-four-week-old pup scrutinizes the author.

Mom and pups at a leisurely moment.

ON THE HUNT

The film shooting went well, with the wolves cooperating wonderfully. Having spent spring 1986 living with this pack, I could build on that experience. I knew just what I could do and what I could not. At times, I lay right up around the den entrance with pups playing around me. Mom didn't care. Many times I was within a foot or so of her pups, while she was a few yards or more away. I grew even closer to this pack and continued to gather data about it. Almost everything we wanted to do worked.

The most difficult problem, I knew, would be watching the pack hunt again. Trying to stay with them on hunts was so time-consuming that I would be missing much good material from around the den. Nevertheless, I had to devote some time to it.

I had been able to observe several incidental wolf/musk ox interactions during both 1986 and 1987. However, I saw few from start to finish that involved most of the pack. And except for the 1986 attack described earlier, all had been unsuccessful.

Of course, that is how it usually is. With any of the wolves' main prey, a successful hunt is the exception. Adolph Murie had documented that principle with wolves hunting Dall sheep and caribou in Mt. McKinley National Park (now Denali National Park), Alaska, in 1944. Only a small fraction of the hunts he watched were successful.

My first wolf study, on Isle Royale, had yielded specific numbers on how most moose hunts end up. Isle Royale is a 210-square-mile island in northern Lake Superior. During the winters of 1958–59, 1959–60, and 1960–61, I had observed from an air-craft while a wolf pack, usually numbering fifteen or sixteen, hunted moose. To catch a moose, of course, wolves first must find one, and even though a moose is a gigantic creature—the largest of the wolf's prey—it inhabits heavily forested areas. Wolves therefore sometimes pass right by moose if the wind is in the wrong direction.

The details of the way the wolf-versus-prey game is played can be seen very clearly from the Isle Royale study. The numbers of wolves and moose living there varies each year. During my tenure on the island, a total of about twenty-three wolves had to make their living trying to catch individuals from a herd of about six hundred moose.

The wolves' problem: Find a moose, catch up to it, try to overcome its defenses—size, weight, power, strength, endurance, and aggressiveness—and kill it, without themselves succumbing. Their solution: Hunt far, wide, and long, scan the entire island, try to catch any moose they can, leave the ones that run too long or fight too hard, and attack those that don't. The result: The relatively few moose that are older, underweight, malnourished, heavily parasitized, sick, injured, or otherwise debilitated are found, dispatched, and eaten.

Here are the figures. Of 131 moose that I watched the large Isle Royale wolf pack detect, usually by odor rather than by sight or tracking, 11 discovered the wolves first and left; 120 did not. Of those, 24 stood their ground and fought the wolves when first encountered; the wolves then always gave up the attempt within five minutes of skirmishing, and the moose remained safe. Some 96 moose fled, however, when the wolves approached, and 43 escaped before the wolves caught up. The wolves did catch up with 53, and of those, 12 stood and fought, and they escaped. Forty-one moose continued to run when the wolves caught up, and of those, 34 outran or outlasted the wolves and also escaped. However, 7 of the moose that ran were attacked, and 6 of them were killed; only one escaped after being wounded.

With wolves hunting deer, their smallest consistent hoofed prey, the situation seems similar, although I haven't put all the figures together yet. Most deer don't stand their ground, however, except if they reach open water during summer or the open rapids of a river in winter.

Because it takes so much searching, hunting, and chasing to find an individual they can kill, each wolf pack must cover a large territory, and each wolf must be able to travel long distances. Where there are more prey animals, the territories are smaller, and where there are fewer, territories are larger. In Minnesota, for example, where deer are the main prey of the wolf, there are around two hundred deer for every wolf; territories average about one hundred square miles per pack.

The farther north you go, in general, the lower the prey density, so the larger the wolf packs' territories are. In Denali Park, Alaska, wolf territories range around six hundred to eight hundred square miles each. In the High Arctic, I'm not yet sure how large the wolf pack's territory is, for that takes more study and technology than I have been able to apply. However, I do have evidence that it is at least one thousand square miles in extent.

The main prey of our wolves are musk oxen and arctic hares, and these animals must scrounge widely in order to find enough vegetation to survive. Neither prey animal is common enough on the vast bleak expanses to support many wolves. One day I was able to catch a ride in a military helicopter and get some idea of the density of musk oxen in our wolf pack's territory. It came out on the order of about one ox per five square miles.

One problem for the wolves, however, is that musk oxen do not come scattered evenly, one every five square miles. Rather they live in herds varying in size up to about thirty individuals. Thus if the average musk ox herd size is ten, there may be an average of only one herd per fifty square miles. This makes quite a difference when you're trying to find them.

A second problem wolves have to overcome in hunting them is the musk oxen's movements. To find enough food, and no doubt also to make it harder for the wolves to locate them, musk oxen are always on the move. A herd grazing in a certain place one day may be resting many miles away the next. Thus when the wolves decide to try to locate some musk oxen, it isn't useful to rely on their own experience. Instead it appears they just strike out on a long foray that may take them days before they actually locate prey they can kill.

That's the way it appeared on July 31, 1987. Jim, who had been taking the early morning watch on the wolf pack around the den, suddenly appeared in our camp a quarter mile away from the den just as I was fixing breakfast.

"Something's up!" he blurted. "I think they're going on a big musk ox hunt. They've been sleeping all night, and now the whole pack has headed out to the north. It really looks like they're serious. We should follow them."

I wanted to accompany the pack on their hunts as much as possible for several reasons. First, it would give me critical information about just how this pack survives on this island with such a low prey density. Second, I really wanted to see how they hunt, how far they must travel to do so, and just where they go. Third, we needed to film as many hunts as we could for the TV documentary. The more hunts we witnessed, the greater the chance we might see a kill, which would be the highlight of our filming.

I had been extremely lucky in 1986, when the herd of fourteen musk oxen, including three calves, had wandered to within a mile of the den and I had watched the wolves successfully attack them. However, I had long known that when it comes to watching wolves hunt, the best way to make luck happen is to observe them in the process as frequently as possible. Sooner or later they have to kill something, so I needed to be as persistent as they were.

During the two summers, I saw several other wolf/musk ox encounters, all of them unsuccessful. The first one, I'll have to say, was quite disappointing. It was on July 9, 1986, about 10:45 P.M., and I was watching five members of the pack chase some hares. Suddenly they sensed a group of three musk oxen a half mile away, grazing on a wet hummocky area. The pack was definitely interested, for they

Mom and Alpha Male, atop the den, watch for intruders.

headed right toward the herd.

There is not much sneaking to be done on the barren ground because of the lack of cover. Nevertheless, it seems the wolves still try to minimize their chances of being discovered, for they go through a stalking phase when approaching musk oxen, during which they move very slowly and deliberately toward the herd, keeping their eyes fixed on it. Presumably they are sizing up the situation and perhaps looking for a stray individual they might rush before it can gain the increased safety of the herd. Or they might be trying to tell if there is a particular vulnerable member, such as an injured one or a calf.

In this case, the musk oxen detected the wolves when they were about one hundred yards away. However, they remained nonchalant about it. The wolves lay down, while the oxen grazed twenty-five to fifty feet apart. Perhaps these particular animals had confronted the others before, for neither group seemed that interested in the other.

It takes a large number of musk oxen, probably at least twenty, to form a circle, so all I ever saw were defensive lines or semicircles. Even two or three musk oxen will stand tightly together and face the wolves, constantly shifting around to minimize attacks on their vulnerable rumps.

I'm not sure what the plan was on this cold, overcast night. However, some of the wolves seemed to go to sleep, and it looked like they were just going to keep the group on edge till someone got tired of the whole situation and decided to move. In this case, the strategy worked to the musk oxen's advantage. One of the wolves soon spied a hare on the horizon and headed after it. A couple of others followed. Soon the three wolves were engaged in a serious attempt to capture the hare.

When their hare hunt was unsuccessful, one of the other wolves drifted off while the other remained sleeping around the musk oxen. About twenty minutes later, she too gave up, and the musk oxen eventually resumed grazing. I felt disappointed that the wolves and musk oxen didn't mix it up more. Still, I realized that it is in both species' interests to minimize energy expenditures and thus to wait until conditions are appropriate to exert themselves.

The TV photographers and I watched a similar encounter between two males from our pack and a herd of eight musk oxen. We first noticed the situation on topping a large mountain and spotting the herd in defense formation on a little plateau about a half mile away. Hills arose in front of the plateau, obscuring each end of it, with the middle holding the musk oxen. The whole scene seemed like a magnificent stage, with me sitting in the balcony. As soon as I realized that the herd was in a defense formation, I knew there must be wolves with them. Sure enough, we soon saw two adult males from our pack lying down about one hundred yards in front of them. Following is a chronology from my field notes of what happened during the next two hours:

10:15 — One wolf arose and went around west and north of the musk oxen and approached them from the north, and the musk oxen tightened their group. There were seven adults and one calf in the middle.

10:18 — One musk ox lay down.

10:20 — One wolf headed north around musk oxen.

10:25 — Two musk oxen lay down.

10:32 — The south wolf approached the herd to within about one hundred feet and then went around to the north.

10:33 — All musk oxen lying.

10:34 — Both wolves give up and head north, then east.

10:50 — Calf stands up.

10:54 — All lying; wolves around one and a half miles east of musk oxen.

11:04 — Two wolves disappearing around one mile east of us. (We were about one-half mile east of musk oxen.)

11:12 — Musk oxen still lying.

11:39 — One musk ox standing.

11:45 — Calf stood for one minute.

11:46 — Two adults standing.

11:50 — One large musk ox moves one hundred feet north and looks and lies down at top lip of ridge.

12:00 — Musk oxen started to leave hill.

12:13 — Musk oxen grazing within one hundred feet of hill. We left.

This was not a spectacular observation by any means. It does show, however, that when wolves drop in on a musk ox herd, the effect is long-lasting even if the wolves soon leave. It took the herd almost two hours after the confrontation to resume their feeding.

Another time I saw two single wolves encounter

A long-tailed jaeger readily accepts a crumb from the author.

an adult musk ox that happened to wander by the pack's rendezvous site. Mom was intently carrying something that she seemed to want to cache when she came up over a rise and confronted the musk ox. She stopped and looked at the ox, and the two just stood about one hundred feet apart staring at each other for a few seconds. Mom then resumed her task, and the musk ox continued on.

Meanwhile, a yearling wolf that was tracking Mom also came upon the musk ox. Probably because it lacked the experience that had told Mom not to fool with the animal, the yearling headed straight toward it. The ox, however, was not about to tolerate any such impudence, based on naiveté or not. It quickly charged the yearling and thereby provided some of the experience the wolf needed.

On another occasion, I did not actually witness the encounter, but saw the aftermath. I had been flying around in a helicopter trying to find the wolves some fifteen miles from the den when suddenly there they were below, three very dirty wolves picking their way along a muddy creek bed in a large open flats. About a mile away, hurrying in the opposite direction, was a herd of about eight musk oxen appearing intent on lengthening the distance between them. My distinct impression was that the wolves had just lost an extensive encounter with them.

Thus it was not with real high expectations that we started out to follow the wolves on July 31. One thing we did realize, however, was that if we were to do the job right it might be quite awhile before we'd return to camp. We threw together as much food and water as we thought we might need and lots of warm clothing, filled the fuel tanks of our ATVs, and headed off to try to find the wolves. By now they had about a thirty-to-forty-minute head start on us.

Our idea was to take the easiest terrain that led generally in the direction the wolves had been heading, stop for a few moments on the highest hills along the route, and scan the area with binoculars where we thought the wolves should be. With the wolves' perhaps three-or-four-mile head start and a series of mountains along their route, we would really have to press the search until we caught sight of them, at least the first time, and confirmed their direction. Then eventually we might be able to get ahead of them or at least into a position to keep track

of their travels.

At first the going was tough, for we had to pick our way over an area of very large tundra hummocks and up and down a series of creek beds and ravines. Finally we emerged on top of a large, bald, gravely hill where the going was very easy, so we made good time. Several times we stopped and scanned the area to our left, where we expected the wolves to be. Finally I spotted them just disappearing up a valley behind a mountain about a mile and a half straight away, all except Mom, who no doubt had returned to the den to look after the pups, as usual.

We took off immediately in their direction, angling up a large mountain toward where the wolves were headed, hoping at least to top the mountain and catch another glimpse of them. I was heartened by the fact that we had been able to catch up with the wolves and spot them.

It took longer than I had expected to reach the summit of the mountain, for it was quite steep and treacherous. When we did, we finally managed to spot the wolves several miles ahead on an extensive open flat bearing a few shallow ponds and a couple of steep river ravines. I realized that if we did not quickly catch up with the pack, we might easily lose them in those ravines.

Way off in the distance, perhaps six miles away, I could see a herd of about eight musk oxen grazing along the flat. The wolves were about two miles from them and homing right in. We were still stuck on the north end of the mountain, trying to figure out a safe way down its steep slope and to plot our general route to the action. Probably we couldn't get there in time, but it was worth a try.

The going was better than expected, but we were still too late. The musk oxen had run off, and whatever skirmish there may have been was over by the time we arrived. The wolves too were gone, so my partner and I split up to find them. It would not be easy, for there were no high spots. We did have the advantage of ATVs and two-way radios, however, and they served us well. The photographer and I lost track of each other after about fifteen minutes.

"On the east side of the steep riverbank," crackled my radio suddenly. Jim had found them! I zoomed over to a raw yellowish riverbank toward where he had disappeared, found a spot to cross the river, and picked my way along until I found a place to climb to the top of the bank.

Suddenly I saw them. The five wolves were traveling up a gentle slope toward three musk oxen, two large and one medium-sized, which had seen them and were standing their ground. The photographer already had his camera set up off to one side and was rolling. What he saw through his viewfinder, however, must have been disappointing. The wolves went right up to the three shaggy beasts and lay down.

The middle-sized ox wedged itself tightly between its companions, and they just stook there, looking somewhat bored. So too the wolves. So too the photographer. I stopped where I was so as not to upset the natural serenity, for suddenly I was superfluous. Through binoculars I tried to make some good scientific observations. But there was not much to be seen. As with other interactions between wolves and musk oxen, this was pretty tame.

Eventually a few of the wolves arose, however, and the musk oxen shifted around nervously. With only three, they really couldn't protect their rear ends, and that's what the wolves seemed interested in. The wolves circled around behind, and the musk oxen whirled. More circling, and more whirling. Suddenly the musk oxen panicked and fled, and the wolves shot after them. Whenever the wolves would nip at their heels, though, the oxen would stop and group up again.

All of the musk oxen seemed to know just when one had been hit too closely by a wolf. I wondered whether there was some sort of sound they uttered when a wolf nipped them, for even the forwardmost ox would instantly stop when a wolf got too close to the rear one.

The attack, which lasted from about 12:45 to 1:00 P.M., continued like this, with the musk oxen trying to remain grouped up, usually on a little rocky knoll that protruded out of the slope, and the wolves trying to get them running. Once when the musk oxen stopped, the wolves rushed in, but one of the larger oxen quickly charged them and dampened their enthusiasm. Finally the wolves seemed to tire of the attack. I really doubt that they drew any blood. The long, dry, shaggy fur of the musk oxen was probably all they tasted.

After several minutes of such skirmishing, the wolves flopped down on a knoll a bit above the herd and fell asleep. The musk oxen too were tired, tongues hanging out and short breaths bursting from their nostrils. The three shaggy beasts remained standing 150 feet down the slope from their adversaries, shifting weight regularly while they pressed together.

Eventually, their shifting increased, and after a few minutes, they began ambling. Gradually their pace increased. We could see that they were trying to steal away. The wolves noticed it too, and the alpha pair arose and half-heartedly started towards them. However, this new charge was only token; the pair quickly aborted it. The pack then continued to rest for another forty-five minutes.

We took our cue and broke out lunch, handfuls of various mixtures of high-energy foods: raisins, nuts, sunflower seeds, and such. Dessert was granola bars, and all was washed down with gulps of "arctic-ade," a vitamin-C-laced powdered fruit drink. This menu was not really a connoisseur's delight, but it was highly practical and allowed quick mobility.

When we were around camp, we actually cooked, both before retiring and on awakening. Our culinary handiwork involved boiling water over a one-burner gasoline stove and skillfully pouring the water into aluminum foil packets of several varieties of dehydrated food: salisbury steak, chicken and noodles, cabbage rolls, ravioli, salisbury steak, chicken and noodles, cabbage rolls, ravioli, salisbury steak, chicken and noodles, cabbage rolls, ravioli, and so on. The secret of enjoying this menu was simple—starvation. It certainly is true that when hungry enough, one can enjoy eating almost anything.

Part of the pack hesitates as the wolves prepare to head out hunting.

SURVIVAL OF THE FITTEST

Finally the wolves arose from their siesta and resumed traveling. Now we would have no trouble staying with them unless they took us to some precipitous gorge or over some soupy mud flat. I knew of neither ahead, so was quite confident. The approach now was similar to that I have used during all my wolf studies while in aircraft watching wolves hunt. We tried to stay far enough ahead of the wolves and off to one side; that way, our presence would not affect them and we could see any prey before the wolves themselves detected it. I would be able to observe the behavior of both prey and predator before either knew of the other's presence.

The terrain ahead was ideal for that: medium-sized rolling hills interspersed with U-shaped glacier valleys, a few shallow lakes, and green flats. Some of the passes were right out of the Old West: weathered, rocky faces and huge, loose sandstone boulders surrounded by sand.

As the wolves streamed through one such pass, they excitedly checked out all the protrusions and marked them, lifting a leg and urinating on them, and defecating in various places. After they left, I examined the area and found several old scats, indicating that these wolves or perhaps some others had marked there several times before.

Wolf scent-marking is a fascinating phenomenon, and although I have studied it for several years both in captive wolves and in the wild, I have yet to fully understand it. I have learned that there are several types of marking, but the easiest to study is one involving raised-leg urination, or RLU. Any-

one who has owned a dog is familiar with such marking, since dogs generally tend to RLU on fire hydrants, trees, car tires, corners of snowbanks, and other conspicuous points in the neighborhood. (I once observed a dog RLUing on an unsuspecting old farmer's pant leg on a street corner in a quaint Italian village!)

Adult high-ranking wolves, both male and female, also RLU. They begin marking as they mature, either when dominant in the social hierarchy or when there is no other competition of the same sex. The latter applies specifically to dispersing wolves who have found a member of the opposite sex and an area that is vacant of other wolves yet that supports enough prey to make a living.

When a dispersing wolf leaves a pack in an area saturated with other wolves, it travels among the other pack territories without marking, presumably to minimize sign of its presence. Obviously the wolf urinates, but instead of urinating every two or three minutes like a marking wolf does, it may save its urine for hours at a time and then discharge it all at once. Low-ranking wolves in captivity often urinate in ponds, again presumably to minimize sign of their presence. Thus I believe that wolf urine can be construed as a challenge to same-sexed competitors.

However, when a dispersing lone wolf finds a vacant area and a member of the opposite sex, then both begin marking together at a very high rate. First one and then the other moves a few yards and repeats the performance. This ritual is also known in other canids and it appears to promote pair-bonding — canid matrimonial vows, so to speak. It is rele-

Alpha Male lifts his right leg to scent-mark in some sort of demonstration related to his feeding on a hare.

vant that old established pairs double-mark at a much lower rate than newly formed pairs.

After a pair is bonded and settles in an area, its urine and feces tend to mark most conspicuous points in strategic locations around the territory, for example, junctions of trails, well-used travel routes, kill scenes, dens and rendezvous sites, and territorial boundaries. My studies in Minnesota with graduate student Roger Peters indicated that the marking rate around the edge of a territory is about double that in the center. Thus through scent-marking, the pack recognizes its own territory, and strangers generally know enough to stay out unless desperate to find food. Wolves also mark their food caches with urine after emptying them. This may save them trouble later when searching for full caches.

All this seems quite clear, but the precise role of individual odor and scent-marking in social interac-

tions among pack members still needs further study. Does scent-marking tell one pack member where another has been? Does it inform other members what an individual has eaten, and when? Our chemical anlayses of urine indicate that there are urine compounds that do contain such information, especially about when a wolf has eaten last.

Whatever the meaning, the wolf pack certainly found it important to mark the arid pass through which we were following them. They then headed off sprightly up the valley while we remained above and ahead of them, trying to anticipate which way they were going. After another couple of miles, I thought we might see a kill. A large lone musk ox, presumably a bull, was grazing on a hillside when the wolves approached. We found a good spot to set up cameras and prepared for the encounter.

Within a minute or two the wolves spotted the

108

huge, dark beast and headed for it. However, like so many moose I have seen, the creature stood its ground and defied the wolves. They circled around it cautiously while it continued to try to face them with lowered head. The wolves quickly lost interest.

Had I not watched this type of behavior so many times before with other prey, I might have concluded that the wolves simply weren't serious—they just weren't hungry. I have heard other biologists characterize this type of seemingly cursory attempt in this way. However, the wolves sure seemed hungry and serious just an hour or two before while harassing three musk oxen. And in my other studies I have watched a pack make a kill shortly after abandoning a previous attempt. The only logical explanation to me is that the abbreviated attempts merely represent ready realization that a paricular prey animal is currently invulnerable. Certainly an ability to read such important information is not too great a mental capacity for an animal whose sole profession is hunting.

Whatever the case, the pack soon continued up a shallow valley toward a pass. Again we were ahead of them, and fortunately we were. As we headed over the pass, we broke out into a lower area. Straight ahead ran a long bench sloping gradually upward to our right to another range of hills a half mile away. To our left, the far shore of a frozen fjord formed the horizon, a bank of rolling mountains with a prominent glacier spilling toward the fjord. On our side of the fjord the area was lower. A little shallow lake lay ahead and to our left, and a broad, rocky draw dropped slowly to a lovely green, wet meadow along the near end of the lake—lush by High Arctic standards.

There in the meadow, peacefully grazing on the sedges, was a herd of about fifteen musk oxen, including calves. The only other time I had seen the wolves make a kill involved a similar herd, and I knew from my other wolf studies that young-of-the-year are prime targets for wolves in summer. In some areas they represent the only segment of the population that can be killed during summer. For example, in northeastern Minnesota, where one of my associates and I had radio-collared more than three hundred deer, about the only adult the wolves ever killed in summer was one that had wandered into a wolf rendezvous site. On Isle Royale, most of the moose the wolves killed in summer were calves.

I believe there are two reasons why calves and fawns form the bulk of the wolves' summer diet. The first is obvious: They are weaker and easier to kill. The second reason is more complex. The actual condition of young animals results from the combination of their genetic heritage and the nutrition they obtain from their mothers, both before and after birth.

First, each newborn represents a unique combination of genes—except for twins or triplets, which may be genetically identical—that has never been tested. In addition, the welfare of the young animal, which is naturally weak and inexperienced, depends critically on the quality and quantity of food it gets. For example, a fawn that goes a day without eating suffers more, nutritionally, than an adult. The combination of the genetic factor and the nutritional factor means that the crop of young includes individuals with great differences among them in condition and fitness.

And, as we all know from Charles Darwin, it is the fittest that survive. After constant testing by various agents in their environment, such as weather and wolves, some of these young animals survive to breeding age and get to pass on their genes, and the process continues. The less fit are the failures in the survival experiment, and they do not get to pass on their genes.

There is a bit more to the fitness problem, however, than just the genes and nutrition of the calves. The fitness of the adults plays an important role too. Whether it be musk oxen or deer or any other wolf prey, the adults who have invested their genes in their offspring possess several methods of helping protect their investment. Deer generally hide their fawns in thick forest, often where wolves would have less chance of finding them—for example, on peninsulas or islands, or near lake shores. Wolves can only come from certain directions then, rather than from 360 degrees. Wiser, more experienced does tend to know how to protect their fawns better, and their genes get passed on.

Caribou bear their helpless calves in isolated, precipitous terrain, like high mountain ridges covered with snow, where wolves must spend more time searching. Then, when the calves can run fast enough, the caribou cows assemble them in large "nursery herds," which move constantly, again

In a typical greeting ceremony, Alpha Male leads the pack toward a meeting with Mom, who is returning to the den area.

maximizing the time the wolves need for finding them. When the wolves do locate a herd, the sheer numbers of fleet caribou tend to confuse the wolves and reduce the chances that any individual calf will be caught.

Moose just stand and fight. There is not much more aggressive an animal than a cow moose with a newborn calf. I found that out one day in Alaska when I tried to place a radio collar on such a calf. Our helicopter had chased off "Mama" and dropped me off to tackle her twenty-five-pound pride and joy. I was straddling the ungainly creature behind a bush while the chopper took my partner to pursue my calf's twin. Suddenly mother appeared, mane hairs raised, eyes blazing, and swinging her head, looking for junior. I was sitting on him, stroking his head gently and saying to myself, "Nice little moose; I won't hurt you; please don't bawl; please don't call mother over charging, with her front hoofs flailing."

Finally the chopper had whirled back over, seen my plight, and headed for the strident cow to scare her away. Knowing that wolves had been killed by those sharp, heavy hooves, I heaved a sigh of relief, placed the collar on my calf, and released it.

I knew that musk ox cows were just as feisty in defense of their calves. The calves run instantly into the mass of gathering adults when wolves approach, and they gain the protection of the entire herd as they huddle in the center of the defensive ring.

I was about to watch this grand experiment at work. The prospect would be exciting to anyone, it seemed to me, although of course I knew it really would not be for the faint-of-heart. Some people would fret at the confrontation about to take place. I was reminded of my mentor Durward Allen's quote of an elderly woman watching a dog kill a cat: "Lord, why can't they be nice!"

My wolves were not about to be nice. Unless, of course, one thinks about it from the viewpoint of their hungry pups, for whom they were about to risk their lives to obtain food. The pack was now twenty miles from their den; they had traveled thirty miles so far this day and tested several musk oxen. Mom was back with the pups, snoozing away, no doubt, perhaps wondering when the rest of the pack would finally return with food. This pack had genes to pass on, too, in the form of five furry figures pa-

110

Alpha Male greets Mom, while Scruffy and Shaggy begin crouching in submission.

tiently playing and resting around the monolith sheltering their den.

To a biologist who was decidedly not faint-of-heart, the impending confrontation brought surges of adrenalin.

"This could be it," whispered Jim excitedly as he situated his tripod.

"There are at least three calves," I replied.

The musk oxen were oblivious to us and the wolves, which were just now coming to where they could see the herd. The photographer began rolling the camera as the musk oxen, a couple hundred yards away, were "being nice" down on the verdant flat. They were spread over a few acres, grinding up the sedges with their massive molars, trying to store fat for the long winter to come. Two calves playfully butted heads, simulating the serious ritual they would eventually repeat many times as giant bulls competing for females to pass on their genes—if they were fit enough to survive.

Even if the wolves did not make a kill today, we would still get to film the musk oxen forming their defensive pattern. I'm not sure who was more tense, the wolves or us. The instant the wolves spotted the dark forms in the valley below, they froze. Musk oxen may not be able to see very well, for we—five wolves and two humans—were all out in the open only 150 yards or so from the herd, yet the oxen still had not noticed us.

If wolves actually think, then they must have known the musk oxen would have less of a chance of seeing them if they moved slowly. Each wolf, still upright, not crouched, crept forward on point slowly and deliberately. It seemed to me that this all would have made more sense had the wolves been sneaking through some thick underbrush or tall grass. But out there on the barren ground they must have stuck out openly. Nevertheless, each animal gradually inched forward for about two minutes.

Suddenly the alpha pair shot forward. The jig was up! The musk oxen quickly gravitated together while the whole wolf pack charged. The wolves swarmed around the swirling herd but were unable to grab a loose calf. Still the herd seemed unnerved. I later wondered whether it was because they were in such a low spot. Other musk oxen I had seen harassed by wolves seemed to want to get up on high ground. For whatever reason, just as the

111

Shaggy, and especially Scruffy, submit to Alpha Male.

wolves appeared to be giving up on this herd, the oxen started heading uphill. Instantly the wolves darted in, catching the herd on a steep uneven slope. This time the wolves appeared inspired. They charged right into the panicked herd, and the herd kept running, with scattered members spread out across a broad front, scrambling uphill and trying to keep their footing.

The wolves chased, and the herd ran. It was hard to keep track of things. Then I noticed one of the wolves homing in on a calf and grabbing at it in flight. The calf dropped back, and for a moment its mother hesitated. However, the herd continued on, now up a more gentle slope, with the wolves constantly darting in and out and charging them. The musk ox cow was torn between trying to save her calf and seeking the safety of her retreating herd. She chose the herd.

The calf was now on its own with Alpha Male attached. The pair floundered around over a ridge almost out of our view for awhile. Meanwhile, uphill from us another drama was unfolding. The wolves had grabbed a second calf and were dragging it away from the herd. Now, however, the herd was

on higher, more level ground, and it was grouping up. A cow charged out of the herd and challenged the wolves tearing at her calf.

The wolves let up for a moment, and the calf shot toward the herd. Again the wolves grabbed it, but again the cow beat off the wolves as both oxen neared the safety of the herd. The wolves dashed in once more and made another try for the calf just as it began intermingling with the adults. The cow joined in the group again, and the wolves came flying out. Too big a risk. It's a great wonder to me how the wolves escaped unhurt. Sometimes they don't. At various times during both 1986 and 1987 I noticed the wolves limping, or bearing wounds that probably came from getting hooked by the sharp recurved horns of musk oxen. The photographer once found near our den a wolf skull that had the tip of a musk ox horn actually embedded on the inner side of its lower jaw. Evidently an ox hooked the wolf hard and broke the tip off, and it just healed over.

Remains of four other wolves have been found that probably were killed by musk oxen. One of these apparently had sustained a blow to the right

112

Alpha Male acknowledges Scruffy's submission with a muzzle bite, which seems to consummate the interaction.

side of its head, for its lower jaw had been broken in two places. Four broken left ribs at a different stage of healing indicated that the poor wolf probably had also been kicked again later.

In my Minnesota study area, I found a somewhat similar situation. One alpha male wolf I had radioed appeared to have been kicked in the head by a deer, for a deer-hoof-shaped section of his skull was caved in. The animal also had three broken ribs that had healed sometime earlier. Another wolf in my study area was once gored by a deer's antlers. And in one summer, two of my radioed wolves were killed by moose in separate incidents.

So clearly wolves take chances every time they tangle with large prey or their offspring. Thus cutting the musk ox calf out of this running herd was an excellent strategy, and it served the pack well. As soon as the herd had regrouped on a high and level spot, the pack again gave up. Suddenly Mid-Back realized that Alpha Male had nailed a calf and was still working on it. The wolf shot straight for the struggling pair and joined in, grabbing the calf by the head.

The calf bucked, bolted, and bellowed, and that brought the rest of the pack. Each new wolf also went for the head, and they all just hung on. Once the calf bucked hard enough to throw all the wolves and took off. But one wolf grabbed it by a back leg, and the others piled on its head again.

Why wolves bite prey on the head is still unknown. I first saw it on Isle Royale, when wolves would grab moose by the nose. Usually one wolf held the nose while the other pack members tore at the moose's rump. The nose wolf stretched way out, tugging and pulling and avoiding the lethal front hooves of the moose. Meanwhile, the other wolves did the real damage. In one case, I watched the moose raise its head and lift the nose wolf right off the ground and swing it from side to side.

With the few musk ox kills I have seen, the first wolf tries to grab the animal by the nose, and the second by the ear. No doubt these areas provide a good grasp, and on musk oxen they may be more certain holds than elsewhere on the body, which is covered by so much long, scraggly hair. A head or nose hold would not seem to be lethal in any way, and in fact, it does take several minutes for the prey to die.

With the social niceties over, the pack heads for the den, with Mom nuzzling Alpha Male.

However, there may be more to it all than that. Farmers control bulls via a nose ring, and I am told that horses can be managed by the nose. I once saw a caribou biologist place his fingers inside the nose of a tame caribou in order to handle it. Now it turns out that laboratory rats that are grabbed by the nose have increased levels of a morphine-like brain hormone that may calm the animal and serve to minimize pain during traumatic times — an advantage for both the predator and the prey.

If this all applies also to musk ox calves, then our subject must have gotten a pretty good dose. I'm really glad I was inured to predators killing prey, because this was pretty strong stuff — the struggling, the bleating, the constant tugging and pulling at the head and face. It's all part of nature, though, and it goes on all over the world every day. That's the way so many animals make their living, and I feel privileged to have watched it close up.

I don't really know just when the calf died, even though it was only about seventy-five feet away. The wolves just kept tugging at its head, and it kept resisting for perhaps five more minutes. Then it fell. But the wolves continued tugging at it. The calf might have been dead at that time. All I could tell is that the wolves gradually tore tufts of hair from it and eventually began working at its undersides and pulling long lengths of gut out.

The whole pack gathered around the calf, each animal hungrily grabbing at the bonanza from a different direction. No telling how long they had gone without a decent meal. Certainly many hours, perhaps days. Wolves can live for weeks without eating. Dogs have been experimentally fasted for as long as 116 days and have still been able to recover.

It's truly feast or famine for wolves. They must be able to withstand long periods without eating because it is so hard for them to find prey they can kill. Most of their life can be summed up by the simple but critical pattern of travel, search, hunt, rest, travel, travel, rest, search, hunt, travel, kill, eat, travel, rest, search, hunt, and so on. Thus most of the time they are hungry. But they can tolerate that hunger, and certainly they must not grow too weak or they would be unable to kill prey when they finally find it.

For now it was feast. Wolves can consume as much as twenty pounds of meat at a meal, and I sus-

114

Alpha Male then regurgitates to a pup, possibly without actually bringing up any food. This could be a mere ceremonial gesture.

pect that is what our pack did. Each member tore at a different part of the carcass. They quickly opened the abdomen and began pulling out viscera. Soon individuals were sticking their noses deep inside the carcass and tugging at various goodies. Blood began staining their heads and necks. And much later, when viewing the film of this whole episode, I suddenly discovered what the wolves' masks came from.

I noticed from the film that before killing the calf, the wolves' faces were relatively unstained. After feeding, dark stains appeared on their muzzles, much darker than the blood all over the rest of their heads. The stain almost certainly came from the viscera, probably from the gut or rumen contents: macerated plants and digestive juices. This discovery was not insignificant. It meant that in later years of watching at the den, I could keep close track of each wolf's nose stains and tell each time the pack killed a musk ox.

After about an hour of gorging, drinking from the nearby pond, and washing off in it, some wolves continued to eat, primarily the alphas. At times individuals would rip out great chunks, such as the

lungs, and steal off to cache them. Generally they would head out for several hundred feet, where the other wolves could not see them, scratch away the surface, drop their prize, and cover it over with forward strokes of the top side of their downturned nose.

What I suspect happens is that after the wolves have filled themselves and ingested enough surplus to take back in their stomachs to their pups, each tries to carry off as much additional food as it can to cache. Then, sometime later when they are out hunting again and they fail to make a kill, they can resort to their caches. And of course when they have pups to feed, the caches allow for a more regular food supply.

I also suspect that the alpha pair does most of the caching. This is because they tend to usurp most of the food, at least with a relatively small creature such as this calf. After the first feeding, when each pack member gets its share, the alphas take over the carcass. The other wolves gather near the remains and hang around, but the alphas clearly dominate. If the carcass is large enough, each animal spaces itself, growling and snarling at its neighbor in between

Similarly, Alpha Male regurgitates to one of the adults, again probably without bringing up food.

trying to pull off chunks to take away and eat in peace.

The musk ox calf, however, was just small enough so the alphas could keep command. As the subordinate members approached them, I observed something I don't think anyone has ever seen before, at least in wild wolves around a kill: The subordinates performed an astounding submissive ritual that seemed to have strong elements of homage-paying, begging, or placating.

"Jim, get this!" I blurted half aloud. The photographer started rolling his film instantly and caught the rare moment.

When the subordinates came to within about six feet of Alpha Male, who was standing over the half-eaten carcass, each seemed to be drawn to the leader like a magnet. The subordinate would lower itself, point its nose toward Alpha Male, pull its ears in and its lips back, and continue forward reluctantly, almost as though it had lost control and was being pulled. The closer it got, the lower and more submissive it became. Alpha Male stopped feeding and began to pay attention, more out of duty, it seemed, than because he really wanted to.

"Look at that," I murmured.

The first subordinate, a male, was now within inches of Alpha Male in a very tense half-crouch, head pointed up and wavering. Then the subordinate lifted a front foot and tried to paw Alpha Male around the head.

Alpha Male, lord wolf king of the surrounding one thousand square miles, snapped half-heartedly, and his subject fell to the ground. It was hard to believe. The subordinates acted like tiny pups, yet each was at least three years old and probably more, and they had all just helped kill the musk ox like equals. Now here they were, each a fawning mass of insecurity in the face of their leader.

I still don't really understand it. Why were they so drawn to the alpha? Were they anxious to feed but reluctant to buck the head honcho? Was there some other reason to approach and demonstrate their submissiveness? They often go through a similar, although lower-intensity, ritual on awakening and grouping up for the hunt. However, in this case they seemed much more highly motivated.

Several times the subordinates submitted and let Alpha Male pin them to the ground, or at least threaten to do so, which had the same effect. It was as though they needed to go through this ceremony, even though in this case Alpha Male did not appear to be that interested in involving himself in it. Notably, the alpha female did not deign to go through the ritual; she was quite able to feed alongside Alpha Male without having to grovel.

I noticed this fact another time too. During a couple of experiments I had run, I gave Alpha Male a dead arctic hare. The first time, the alpha female was not there but the other two males were, and they tried to beg parts of the hare from Alpha Male. However, he crunched the whole thing right up in front of them unabashedly, and they never got a piece. The next time I gave him a hare, the alpha female was around. She rushed over and managed to grab pieces away, although she did have to do so forceably. Nevertheless, there was no groveling for her.

With the musk ox calf, the alpha pair continued to feed while the subordinates hung around the edges. I crawled up to within about twenty-five feet to watch the whole show in ringside fashion. Had I tried to get closer, I might have had to grovel a bit myself. Being rusty at groveling, I decided not to test that particular talent.

About three hours after making the kill, two of the five wolves left the scene and started back toward the den. It was about 6:30 P.M., and we had seen and filmed what we wanted to at the kill, so we decided to return to the den also. We wanted to try filming at least some of the wolves when they came home and delivered their bounty to the pups.

Thus we too left and beelined it as best we could for the den. It took three hours, and we had to stop at a fuel cache to refuel. We arrived back at the den about 10:00 P.M., just forty-five minutes before the rest of the pack returned. The usual excited greetings were exchanged, and the pups fed. The pack then all rested and slept, having been on their hunt for about sixteen hours. Needless to say, we did the same.

The inexperienced Scruffy makes a valiant effort to open an adult musk ox.

All he gets for his efforts is a mouthful of shaggy hair.

Alpha Male is far more effective than Scruffy was in his feeding on an adult musk ox.

Mid-Back noses around Alpha Male, hoping to share in his take.

ON KNOWING THE WOLF

As I lay down that night in my tent, reviewing the day's events, I marveled again over how tolerant these wolves were and how much I had been able to learn from them. The nagging thought also intruded. Had I done the right thing? First the magazine article, then the TV documentary, now this book.

To this day I am not certain. I do realize there was no choice. Once having found this pack and their den, and once having acclimated them to us, I was obligated to my expedition sponsors to report the story. After publication of the story, the TV documentary was inevitable, and so too this book. From the strictly personal standpoint, my lifetime dream had come true in a way I could never have imagined. That's hard for anyone to keep quiet, especially when the dream involves living with such a charismatic, photogenic pack of wolves as these.

And that, after all, is the great benefit of the project. There are still too many people in this world who hate wolves. Most would change their minds if they could share my experience. It is true that the tame wolves that a few people raise and take around for school children and legislators to see do help improve the wolf's image. However, those wolves are not the real item. Deliberately raised as pets in a human environment, they do not accurately portray the species. One must understand the wolf in the wild to truly appreciate the animal.

Mom and Alpha Male, Scruffy, the Lone Ranger, Mid-Back, Left Shoulder, and Shaggy know none of this. They go on about their lives, chasing hares, killing musk oxen, raising pups, and when there is some leisure time, merely lying around the tundra hummocks. Hundreds of years ago, probably thousands, their ancestors did the same thing in the same place, the ancient monolith sheltering generation after generation of pups.

Meanwhile, we humans judge these creatures by our own standards. If they kill, they are bad. If they take the old, the young, the sick, and the weak, they are good. If they mate for life, that makes them better. If they kill and eat one of their own, they are ghastly.

However, in their own world, up there in the High Arctic where human standards are sparse, this wolf pack can maybe teach us to think about their species in a different way. By sharing the life of this pack that I have had the extreme privilege of knowing, I hope I can help other people to see the wolf for what it is: one more magnificent species, superbly adapted to contend with its harsh environment, and highly deserving of our understanding and acceptance.

As I prepared to leave the wolves, already planning my return next year, I reflected on the extreme privilege I'd had living with the pack. It was the highlight of my life.

121

WOLF ORGANIZATIONS

The International Wolf Center

The International Wolf Center is a unique concept being developed in Ely, Minnesota, in the heart of wolf range. Ultimately the Center will combine a variety of vibrant wolf-related educational activities into a single setting. It will not be a museum, zoo, school, or conference center, although it will have elements of all of these. The Wolf Center will be a single institution that will provide a mix of wolf-related activities to a mix of people. It will not propagandize for or against the wolf; it will provide factual education about the wolf.

A unique and important part of the Wolf Center currently functioning is a program for the public to experience the wolf in its own environment, via hikes to find wolf tracks, abandoned dens, and other signs; evening trips to hear wolves howl; ski, snowshoe, and dogsled excursions to snowtrack wolves and see remains of kills; and winter flights to actually observe wolves. These activities will enliven the education eventually to be offered by exhibits, lectures, demonstrations, and audiovisual presentations when a building is constructed.

The international component of the Center will be provided by appropriate displays and by periodic visits from foreign wolf specialists, who will present programs about wolves in their countries. Because the wolf originally was the most widely distributed mammal in the world, there is strong international interest in the animal. The Ely area has long been the leader in production of information about wolves, so wolf specialists from many countries regularly visit the area.

The International Wolf Center will include (1) the Science Museum of Minnesota's 8,000-square foot "Wolves and Humans" exhibit, along with a changing temporary display; (2) a captive wolf pack and associated audiovisuals; (3) a strong year-round program of field-oriented activities; (4) regular public audiovisual presentations, demonstrations, and private viewings; (5) on- and off-site instruction to visiting school classes at all levels and to the general public; and (6) permanent storage of wolf information and specimans. Wildlife workshops, symposia, concerts, and other intermittent major functions of international scope will also be planned for the Center.

The International Wolf Center is affiliated with Vermilion Community College, a Minnesota state institution, and it has the endorsement of the Eastern Timber Wolf Recovery Team, the International Union for the Conservation of Nature and Natural Resources' Wolf Specialist Group, and several environmental organizations. The Center is being developed by the Committee for an International Wolf Center, a nonprofit organization of wolf experts, environmentalists, educators, wilderness ecologists, naturalists, and other professional conservationists. The author is vice-chairman of the committee.

The committee's address is:

Committee for an International Wolf Center
c/o Vermilion Community College
1900 E. Camp St.
Ely, MN 55731

Defenders of Wildlife

Defenders of Wildlife is a national nonprofit organization dedicated to the preservation of wildlife and its habitat. One of its primary current projects is to foster wolf recovery in the Rocky Mountains of the U.S. Its address follows:

Defenders of Wildlife
1244 Nineteenth St. N.W.
Washington, D.C. 20036

The IUCN-SSC Wolf Specialist Group

The Wolf Specialist Group is an international organization of authorities on wolves, currently including members from Canada, the U.S., Italy, Sweden, Finland, Norway, Spain, Portugal, Israel, the Soviet Union, Poland, Mexico, and China. The author has been chairman since 1978. The group deals with wolf conservation matters of international significance, especially situations involving endangered populations. As such, the Wolf Specialist Group is one of seventy-seven specialist groups composing the Species Survival Commission (SSC). The SSC in turn is one of six commissions that carry out the main activities of the International Union for the Conservation of Nature and Natural Resources (IUCN).

The IUCN is the foremost international conservation organization, having representatives from 117 countries, including 59 governments, 125 government agencies, 353 national citizen organizations, and 31 international citizens groups. In addition, 700 nonvoting individuals and organizations from 65 countries also support IUCN. Funding for IUCN comes from membership fees, and many of its conservation activities have been financed by the World Wildlife Fund. IUCN functions primarily by setting conservation policies and ideals and urging member governments to adhere to them.

Canadian Wolf Defenders
Box 3480
Station D
Edmonton
Alberta T5L 4J3

123

During off moments, pups may turn any pack member — willing or not — into a plaything.

SUGGESTED READINGS

For readers interested in digging deeper into the life of the wolf, the following books will provide a wealth of solid facts:

Allen, D. L. 1979. The Wolves of Minong: Their Vital Role in a Wild Community. Houghton Mifflin Co., Boston.

Boitani, L. 1987. Dalla Parte del Lupo. L'Airone di Giorgio Mondadori e Associati Spa, Milano.

Gray, D. R. 1988. The Musk Oxen of Polar Bear Pass. National Museum of Natural Sciences, Fitzhenry and Whitside, Markham, Ontario.

Harrington, F. H., and P. C. Paquet (Eds.). 1982. Wolves of the World. Noyes Publications, Park Ridge, N.J.

Klinghammer, E. (Ed.). 1979. The Behavior and Ecology of Wolves. Garland STPM Press, N.Y., London.

Mech, L. D. 1970. The Wolf: Ecology and Behavior of an Endangered Species. Doubleday, Garden City, N.Y.

Murie, A. 1944. The Wolves of Mount McKinley. Fauna of the National Parks of the United States. Fauna Series No. 5. U.S. Government Printing Office.

Peterson, R. O. 1977. Wolf Ecology and Prey Relationships on Isle Royale. National Park Service Scientific Monograph Series No. 11.

Walberg, K. I. 1987. Ulven. Grondahl & Sons, Forlag A.S., Oslo.

Zimen, E. 1981. The Wolf: A Species in Danger. Delacorte, N.Y.

WOLF!

To keep abreast of wolf conservation issues and new factual information about wolves as it appears, subscribe to WOLF! a quarterly news bulletin from Janet Lidle, WOLF!, P.O. Box 112, Clifton Heights, PA 19018 ($15 U.S. per year in U.S.; $20 U.S. per year outside U.S.).

INDEX

Note: The italicized abbreviation "ph." refers to a photo on the referenced page.

Allen, Durward L., 3
Alpha female, 51
    as mother of pups, 51, 61, 64
Alpha Male (name of wolf), *ph.* 53
    behavior to pups, 54, 61
    description, 51, 54
Arctic hare, *ph.* 28
    coloration, *ph.* 28, *ph.* 29
    diet, 27
    ricochetal gait, 27
    wolves' hunting of, 69
Arctic Wild, 15
Arctic wolf, definition, 13
Attack on humans, 15
Bathurst Inlet, 19
Beeline, wolves' use, 37
Brush wolf, 13
Caching of food, 115, 117
Canis latrans, 13
Canis lupus, 13
Canis rufus, 13
Calving (icebergs), *ph.* 21
Caribou, *ph.* 26
    defense mechanisms, 25, 26, 109–10
    diet, 25
    habitat, 25
Coyote, 13
Crisler, Lois and Chris, 15

Defense mechanisms
    caribou, 25, 26, 109–10
    deer, 109
    moose, 110
    musk ox, 110. *See also generally* Hunting, of
        musk oxen
Den, *ph.* 32
    age of site, 92
    author's finding of, 40
    author's search for, 33–40
    location choice, 33
    move to new, *ph.* 44, 45
    second, *ph.* 46
    used only for pups, 54
Dominance
    breeding and, 51
    feeding and, 117
    in pack, 61, 64, *ph.* 111, *ph.* 112, *ph.* 113, 117
Feeding behavior, 71, *ph.* 81–87, 114–15, 117, *ph.*
    118–19. *See also* Food; Regurgitation
Female wolf, physical characteristics, 51
Following the Tundra Wolf (film), 19
Food. *See also* Feeding behavior; Prey animals;
    Regurgitation
    pack relations and, 61
    pup/adult interaction, 58, 60–61, *ph.* 68
Glacier, *ph.* 21
Gray wolf, 13
Greeting, between wolves, *ph.* 110
Grise Fiord, 15
Hare, arctic. *See* Arctic hare

High Arctic
    clothing in, 20, *ph.* 30
    definition, 15
    terrain, 25, *ph.* 34
    travel to, 20
    vegetation, 25
Howling, *ph.* 18
    chorus, 57–58, *ph.* 60
    pups', 58
    significance, 36
Hunting
    of hares, 69
    of moose, 99–100
    of musk oxen, 69–71, *ph.* 72–80, 88–89, 100,
        102, 104–5, 108–9, 111–14
Iceberg, *ph.* 21, *ph.* 24, *ph.* 34
Injuries to wolves, 112–13
Isle Royale National Park, 12, 99–100
Jaeger, long-tailed, *ph.* 103
Jesudasen, Terry and Bezal, 20
Left Shoulder, *ph.* 53
    description, 54
Living with the pack, 45, *ph.* 46, 48
Lone Ranger, *ph.* 55
    description, 54
Long-tailed jaeger, *ph.* 103
Male wolf, physical characteristics, 51
"Mask" on muzzle, *ph.* 55, 92, 94, 115
Media, pack and, 48, 92, 121
Mid-Back, *ph.* 52
    description, 51
    as hunter, 61, *ph.* 65, *ph.* 66
Miller, Frank, 15
Mom, *ph.* 50
    description, 51
Moose
    defense mechanisms, 110
    hunting of, 99–100
Mowat, Farley, 12, 15
Murie, Adolph, 12, 99
Musk ox(en), *ph.* 26
    defense mechanisms, 110. *See also* Musk ox(en),
        hunting of
    diet, 25
    habitat, 25
    hunting of, 69–71, *ph.* 72–80, 88–89, 100, 102,
        104–5, 108–9, 111–14
    population density, 25
    size, 69
National Geographic, 19, 20, 48
Never Cry Wolf, 12, 15
Pack
    structure of, 54
    territory of, 57

Parmelee, David, 15
Peary caribou. *See* Caribou
Play, pups', 58, *ph.* 62
Polar bear, *ph.* 16
Prey animals, 11–12. *See also* Arctic hare; Moose;
    Musk ox(en)
    livestock as, 12
    population density, 25, 100
    young, 109
Pup(s)
    eating, 58, 60–61, *ph.* 63
    howling, 58
    physical characteristics, *ph.* 47
    playing, 58, *ph.* 62, *ph.* 67
    rearing of, 54
    sale of, 12
Raised-leg urination (RLU), 107
Range
    current, 12
    historic, 11
Rearing of pups, 54
Red wolf, 13
Regurgitation, 60–61, *ph.* 63, *ph.* 115, *ph.* 116
Reproduction cycle, 64
Research methods, with wolves, 12, 48
Resolute Bay, 20
Ricochetal gait, arctic hare's, 27
Scent-marking, 107–8
Scruffy, *ph.* 55
    and author's hat, 42, *ph.* 43
    description, 54
Shaggy, *ph.* 52
    description, 51
Sleep, *ph.* 58
Species, wolf and related, 13
Speed, wolf's, 36
Structure of pack, 54
Submission. *See* Dominance
Subspecies, wolf, 13
Territory of pack, 57
Timber wolf, 13
Tracks, wolf, *ph.* 17
Travel with the pack, author's, 29, *ph.* 31
Tundra wolf, 13
Urination postures, 54, 94, 96, 107
Values, human, 121
Wolves of Isle Royale, 15
Wolves of Minong, The, 3
Wolves of Mt. McKinley, The, 12
World of the Wolf, The, 12
Yearling(s)
    appearance, 54, 94
    behavior, 54, 94, 96
    dispersion of, 94, 96

Mom tolerates no nonsense. When a pup acts too independent, she picks it up unceremoniously and carries it back to the den.